The Boss is Dead

Leadership through Influence not Position

Mark Cowper-Smith

The Boss is Dead

Copyright © 2020 Mark Cowper-Smith

Dedication:

It is customary to dedicate a book to those individuals who were instrumental in the writing of the book. These include spouses, friends, editors, agents, contributors, and a host of others.

This dedication is a little different. Shell and I worked on this book together, and together we want to thank all those churches who have received us so graciously and lovingly over the years. You let us road test our leadership theories. We learned as much from you as you may have received from us. Your leadership examples inspired and informed the book. For the sake of your humility [a characteristic of influential leadership] we are not going to list you by name. You know who you are. Thank you for your love and inspiration. We hope to see you again soon!

Special thanks to those who contributed stories that we have included. We appreciate your permission as what you learned, enriched us all.

One last huge thanks. We thank our home church, the Gathering Place Church of San Diego, for making it possible for us to travel and teach as we have for so many years. What a great group of people to share life with!

Reviews:

"I began studying leadership in 1985 due to my ineffectiveness as a general manager. I have been a student of leadership ever since and it is now one of my greatest joys in life. After thirty-five years of reading everything I could get my hands on, Mark's book ranks at the very top. He does a brilliant job at blending the Bible, honest stories, practical insights, and application. A must read if you want to see your influence as a leader substantially increase. "

John Ettore, Lead Pastor Gathering Place Church

Over the years, I have read many books on leadership. I can unequivocally attest that none of them compare to the content found in "The Boss is Dead." Mark bypasses the constant evolution of leadership theory and practice that changes like the wind and focuses on the timeless truth found in God's Word. I pray that we can all lead through influence and grace, free from the shackles of corporate hierarchal structures, ego result-driven models of success, and insatiable appetites for power and prestige that nauseate the ultimate servant leader, Jesus. May this book become foundational to anyone who desires to lead from a place that will never fade away or perish,

Brian Overturf - Senior Pastor of 14 years and current graduate student of Leadership and Spirituality at Vanguard University of Southern California.

Mark Cowper-Smith has created a significant examination of management styles and effectiveness in his book, "The Boss is Dead." He provides viewpoints from both Christian and secular writings to thoroughly examine the impact of positional authority (ruling by title and process) versus a more influential leadership style which may be called a "servant leader" in many business school curriculums. The author challenges the reader to perform self-reflection of major leadership traits and gives concrete examples of how such traits can inspire the workplace and individual relationships when implemented by a servant leader. The author warns that these same traits can be seen as manipulative if used through positional authority to "manage" others. The core lessons hit on the "soft science" of examining how others react to traits such as self-awareness, empathy, and authenticity, and provides a deeper dive into three core areas highlighted through surveys as being most appreciated by people: competence, character and caring. The questions at the end of each chapter provide a great opportunity for digging deeper and applying the concepts individually or in group sessions. The summary of the major concepts in the back of the book is helpful to quickly capture the major concepts for practical application to our lives. This book walks a fine balance between Christian leadership concepts and business leadership concepts taught in major universities, and the lessons will help us become better communicators and influencers in both our business and private relationships.

Les Meredith, Vice President, Ostomy 101 [International Non-profit]

What a refreshing and wonderfully expressed book for leaders. This is a book all leaders should read regardless of their

5

religious belief. It will not only help you achieve your leadership visions and goals, it will also create an environment of productivity.

Some of the traditions the military upholds to show respect for positional authority are saluting, calling the entire room to attention when the boss walks in, and standing in parade rest when talking to a senior ranking sergeant. As a US Army leader, my senior rank (displayed boldly in front of my chest for all to see) is enough to get soldiers to give me respect even before I speak. As Mark has written, this is where positional leadership should end. Up to this point, it has served its purpose. What to do after you've been recognized as the leader is what this book will effectively teach you.

As a US Army First Sergeant of an Engineer Company with over 200 soldiers under my leadership, the principles of this book gave me the tools to help my company achieve missions under hectic and stressful conditions. Bottom line is, anyone who leads with a genuine heart for those they lead will find themselves being respected and obeyed. This book provides a "battle plan" for becoming a leader of great influence.

Phil Williams 1SG US ARMY (Retired)

Table of Contents

INTRODUCTION

Why did I write this book? This book came about because of an epiphany I experienced a long time ago. At the age of 28 I became a follower of Jesus. For me, inviting Jesus "into my heart" was a very disruptive experience. It was as if He shone a flood light into a very dark place. All of a sudden, what I thought was a pretty clean room turned out to be an outhouse. I was shocked at the depth of my selfishness. I had considered myself to need nothing more than some minor adjustments. What I saw revealed the need for a complete renovation.

One of the first revelations, regarding my need for serious change, concerned my manipulation of those around me. What I had taken for "leadership ability" was revealed to be tainted by manipulation and control. The problem was [and—still—is] that I am a dangerous concoction of intelligence and charisma, mixed with good humor and sincerity. It was easy for me to get people to do what I wanted them to do. I never saw this as a bad thing – the boy needed some serious self-awareness.

What does all this have to do with this book? When God revealed to me the depth of my self-centeredness, it truly sickened me. I became hyperaware of every subtle effort to control those around me. I made it my goal to never manipulate anyone to do anything they did not truly want to do. This goal should have excluded me from most positions of leadership, but the opposite happened. I found that people felt safe with me. They granted me great influence in their lives precisely because I did not have a plan for their lives.

When God shone His light into my heart, He poured His love in as well. I found myself loving people in a way I had never imagined possible [or desirable]. My goal for them became God's best [in His opinion] rather than my best [in mine]. I'm

9

not suggesting I achieved this, but at least it was my goal. All of this was lived in the context of my secular employment [lawyer] and later, in leadership within the local church. My dream was to lead a church under grace, as opposed to through any form of command and control [legalism]. And to a great extent, it worked.

Back to the question, why write this book? For reasons that will be explored later, the church has been slow to step away from a positional leadership model. There are historic and theological reasons for this failure to move away from command-and-control hierarchical leadership, but I am quite sure they are faulty. You are invited to be the judge.

This book is a study of two kinds of leadership: leadership through positional authority and leadership through influence. I define positional leadership as authority that is derived principally from the leader occupying a titled position of leadership, with the express understanding that the leader is to be obeyed simply because he or she occupies that organizational position within the group being led. It is the position which must be respected rather than the person.

On the other hand, leadership through influence flows from the person rather than the position and it requires no title or position to assure followership. It is granted voluntarily by those following the leader. It comes from three sources: competence, character and caring.

Here are some of the questions we will address:

- What is our western culture's response to positional authority?
- What are the historic and theological origins of positional authority?
- What is the role of positional authority in the Old Testament?

10

- What are the weaknesses of positional authority evident in the Old Testament?
- How does the New Covenant [grace] affect positional authority in the New Testament?
- What is Jesus' and the Apostle Paul's leadership model?
- What are the sources of influence in a leader's life?
- How can our influence be increased?
- When is positional leadership essential?

When I began the research for this book, I viewed its context as the local church. As my research progressed, I found that the secular world is exploring leadership through influence, to a degree that surprised me. I realized that influence affects all of life's relationships, friendships, marriages, parenting, business, family, neighbors, etc. Humans are herd creatures who both influence, and are influenced by, those around them.

The result of this realization is that this book will be helpful for everyone in whatever relationships they find themselves. The secular research I refer to is very illuminating and exciting.

This book is written from a Christian perspective but the greatest joy I experienced while doing the research for this book came from discovering that the best secular research on influence dovetails perfectly with what the Bible teaches about it. The result is that this book will be helpful for everyone who wants to become a person of influence. And now for a confession...

The title of the book is an overstatement designed to capture your attention long enough to entice you to read the back cover, and perhaps, this introduction. Please forgive my momentary lapse into manipulation.

By saying that "The Boss is Dead", am I saying that there is no room for positional leadership within the church or society? No.

What I am saying is that positional leadership has its place. For the reader who fears this book will be unfair to positional leadership I invite you to skip ahead to Chapter 22 for a discussion of when positional leadership is essential.

The theme of this book is that positional leadership may be a good place to start, but a very bad place to finish. It does not set people free to be all God has destined them to be. It does not empower them as does grace. Not only is it bad for those under it, it tends to warp the character of those who practice it, as our journey through the Bible will make evident.

This is the crux of the matter; positional leadership has its place. There are times when only it will work, but most of the time, influence is a far more effective way to lead. This is what the business world is discovering, as are marriage and family counselors. The annoying irony for me, as a leader in God's church, is that the Bible has provided a road map for us to lead through influence. This road map has existed for almost two thousand years. My fear is that we may be the last to get on board the "influence express."

Not all of us will lead a business, church, marriage or family, but all of us have the opportunity to be influential in someone's life. Reading and applying this book will increase your influence.

I invite you to get on board. It just could be a transforming journey.

SECTION ONE

HOW THE BOSS
CAME TO BE THE BOSS

Chapter 1: The Times They are a Changin'

"Come mothers and fathers throughout the land
And don't criticize what you can't understand
Your sons and your daughters are beyond your command
Your old road is rapidly agin'. Please get out of the new one
If you can't lend your hand for the times, they are a-changin'."

"The Times They are a Changin" – Bob Dylan [1964]

It has been said that this song perfectly captured the spirit of the 1960s. It is a song about change. Those of us who came of age in the '60s have seen some serious change. Let's take some contemporary issues and try to define them in the ethos of the 1950s.

Social media in the '50s was simple – "want" and "for sale" ads in your daily newspaper. Yes, we had telephones. Each home had a black rotary dial telephone. It sat in a central location of the house, exposed to the entire family. There was no such thing as a private phone call. In our home the kids [teenagers] were restricted to five-minute calls!

Internet marketing consisted of the Sears catalogue delivered through the mail, once yearly. Computers existed, but they were the size of a semitruck and were housed in walk-in freezers. They were owned by the government and understood by no one.

"Inflation" meant gas was going from 15 cents a gallon to 16 cents a gallon.

Terrorism was simple – the Chihuahua next door that tried to bite our ankles on our walk home from school.

Speaking of school – school safety meant wearing the correct sneakers to gym class. The biggest problem with misbehavior at school was, and I am not making this up, chewing gum.

"Home Theater" consisted of a 12-inch black and white TV. No remote control, but it didn't matter much because we only received two channels.

And finally, "drugs" meant Aspirin.

And then along came the 1960s.

Everything changed. Much of the change was simply fashion; clothes, long hair and of course the music, but there was change that would last. It would change Western culture permanently. Bob Dylan (a popular songwriter) sang about change, but at a deeper level he was singing about rebellion... "your sons and your daughters are beyond your command." The sad fact is that the song turned out to be prophetic. A deep distrust of authority was birthed in the 1960s which has increased in each generation since. So pervasive was the counter-culture birthed in the '60s that it affected the entire Western world and beyond.

I came of age in the '60s. I remember our parents telling us that our distrust of authority was just a passing stage of our development into adulthood, that like a fashion, it would pass along with our long hair and bellbottom jeans. Teenagers are always rebellious, they said.

They would probably have been correct but for a few seminal events that forever altered our perception of authority. The Vietnam War and the Watergate Scandal dealt a mortal blow to our trust in our government and its leaders. Distrust of leadership was now a part of our world view. As such, we believed we had a moral responsibility to pass it on. This we did when our generation became the teachers of the next. We raised children with a "built-in" distrust of authority, who raised children with an even greater distrust of authority, and on it went until today.

If you have any doubt as to the truth of the statement that we have a problem with disrespect for authority, just talk to any public-school teacher, or google "disrespect for authority" and peruse the articles.

We are inundated with humorous stories about the entitlement mentality of the Millennial generation, to such a degree that we tend to dismiss it as some sort of joke. It is no joke. The extent of the problem revealed itself to me last year at a party. Before I tell you the story, please understand that I am not suggesting that all Millennials disrespect authority. Rather, I am saying that we are experiencing a growing cultural drift in that direction which is more pronounced in this generation than the last. It is a growing problem. Back to my story...

2018

My wife invited me to a Christmas party at the home of a management guru. I of course, knew almost no one, so I lingered around the appetizers until I wore out my welcome and had to find someone to talk to. I found an old guy [like myself] sitting by himself. I sat down and started with the usual questions; what's your name and what do you do? We exchanged names and he told me that he had been in senior management with a large manufacturing firm, but now he is retired and works as a management consultant. I asked him if he had a consulting specialty and he told me that his practice is mostly centered on helping businesses handle their millennial employees. He now had my undivided attention.

I asked him for an example of the kind of issue he would consult on and he told me this story: A small manufacturing firm had hired a 20-something man to load their products onto their delivery trucks. It was a regular 8 hour/day job. One day the young man failed to come in to work. He didn't call with any explanation. He was gone for three days until they finally reached him and asked him to come in right away. When he came in, they asked him why he hadn't come in to work. He told them that he had decided to take a few days off.

They explained to him that the only reason to stay home was because of genuine sickness, and that, at the very least, he should have phoned them. He didn't agree. As far as he was concerned, he had the right to decide when, and for how long, he would work. At this point my new management consultant friend was brought in to deal with the problem.

My new friend met with the young man and went over his reasons for staying home, and why he didn't call his boss to tell him why he didn't come to work. The young man repeated his reasoning adding that, "I just didn't feel like working." When asked why he didn't phone his boss he said that his cell phone battery ran down [they take about two hours to recharge]. My new friend patiently tried to tell him that his work hours are not optional and that calling in is essential. The young man was immune to reason and had to be fired.

I asked my new friend what the solution is to this kind of entitlement/disrespectful behavior. He told me that in most cases there is no solution other than the termination of the "employee."

Growing disrespect for authority

It is arguable that this story is nothing more than anecdotal evidence. Not so, here is a very quick and simple indication of the breadth of the problem. Go to Google and search "research on disrespect for authority" and count the number of results indicated at the top of the page. At the time of writing [a moment ago] I found 6,540,000 results! Here are two very revealing studies:

On January 16th, 2017, Matthew Harrington wrote an article for the Harvard Business Review.[1] In it he quoted the results of the Edelman Trust Barometer which is a survey done with more than 33,000 interviewees in 28 countries. Edelman has been doing the trust survey for 17 years [long before the term "Millennial" came to prominence]. The survey measures the level of public trust in government, business, media and NGOs [non-governmental organizations, usually organized for some humanitarian charitable purpose]. Mr. Harrington notes that for the first time in 17 years the public's trust is down in all four categories. He starts his article by saying, "We are living in an era of backlash against authority."

A deep distrust of authority was birthed in the 1960s which has increased in each generation since.

On January 23rd, 2018, The New York Times published an article by Dhruv Khullar, entitled "Do You Trust the Medical Profession?"[2] He cites very alarming statistics. In 1966 75% of Americans had great trust in their medical leaders. Today it has dropped to 34%. Only 25% of Americans trust the health care system. Is it a matter of chance that trust has dropped steadily since the 1960s? I think not - we have come by our disrespect for authority honestly. We have been taught it, and it is in the cultural air we breathe.

Is the church immune to the cultural drift?

The context for this book is leadership in the local church. It is written by a pastor for fellow leaders in the body of Christ. Because it is a book about church leadership it would be convenient to suggest that because the Bible teaches submission to authority [both secular and religious] we can ignore the problem of disrespect in the world because we are "in the world but not of it."

This conclusion is naïve. The western church today is influenced more by the world than it influences the world. In our book "Reluctantly Supernatural in an Age of Reason"[3], Bob Maddux and I contrast the input the average American Christian receives from the world [secular media] versus the Bible. Our research revealed the following:

Frequency	Minutes/ Bible	Minutes/ Media	Ratio
Daily - 14%	37.67	639	1: 16.96
4 x week - 16%	150.68	4459	1: 29.6
1 x week - 6%	37.67	4459	1: 118.37
1 x month - 6%	37.67	17,838	1: 473.5
3-4 x a year - 7%	150.68	214,056	1: 2841.2
1-2 x a year - 9%	75.34	214,056	1: 5682.4
Never – 27%	0	214,056	1: 214,056

Our best-case scenario for the 14% who read the Bible daily is a ratio of almost 17:1 in favor of the world. For the average American Christian, the ratio is closer to several hundred to one. It is not a stretch to suggest that if our secular culture is having a problem with disrespect for authority, then so is the church. The pastors I have talked to about the problem have confirmed its existence. One pastor friend of mine referred to leading his church as "herding cats." What a great title for this book. Just saying the phrase out loud brings an immediate sense of angst.

The frustration deepens when we consider that the Bible teaches respect and obedience to our God ordained leaders. Yet, this fact creates an additional problem and that is that our response to disrespect is often to demand respect and obedience by virtue of our God ordained position of authority, as taught in the Bible. We want to appeal to the Bible in support of our position of leadership, but in so doing we merely reinforce the perception that we cannot be trusted to preach the Bible without using it to support our vested interest to lead.

In the '60s we called that a "catch 22." If few of our people read the Bible regularly it probably means that they don't use it much for decision making. Perhaps in many of our congregants' lives, the Bible has lost its authority as well.

All the foregoing begs the question; if our position of authority is being disrespected, how do we lead? This may not be an important question for those of us leading churches composed of old-school Christians raised with a respect for their leaders, but for those of us who have any intention of leading the next generation the answer to the question is vital. Millennials compose the next generation the church must learn to lead. Appealing to positional leadership is not going to work to "herd the cats."

At this point in our discussion, it might be helpful to remind ourselves of our definition of the term "positional leadership." Throughout this book, when I use the term positional leadership, I am referring to leadership authority that is derived principally from the leader occupying a titled position of leadership, with the express understanding that the leader is to be obeyed simply because he or she occupies that organizational position within the group being led.

Millennials compose the next generation the church must learn to lead. Appealing to positional leadership is not going to work to "herd the cats."

20

It presupposes a hierarchical leadership structure which is known to all within the organization. It is a pure chain of command leadership structure. In this form of leadership, it is the position which is respected rather than the person occupying the position. The leader would be acting consistently with his authority to say, "Do what I say because I am the boss." No reason for the command is necessary or expected.

The best example we have of positional authority is the military. A commanding officer need only say, "that's an order" and he may assume it will be obeyed. Corporate America has been traditionally organized around the same command structure. I remember asking a past boss why he gave me an unusual order. I was not being disrespectful; I just didn't understand the reason for the order. His answer was short and simple, "Go do it because I sign your paycheck!"

Positional authority is the way the world gets things done. It has always existed throughout history. It is taken as a given. It is hard to imagine any other form of leadership. And now it is under siege, even in the military. I was discussing the subject of this book with a friend of mine who has been in the military for years. I said, "I think the only place where positional authority is still respected is in the military." He said, "Not as much as you might think. If we don't respect the officer above us there are dozens of ways to thwart his orders without getting caught."

This military example brings us to the core problem with positional leadership; **when we do not respect the person in charge, we tend to withhold our best efforts.** This makes perfect sense if you consider the role of motivation on performance. It is a truism to say that motivated employees work harder and are more productive than those who are not motivated. When we combine our present cultural disrespect for positional authority with a positional leader who cannot or will not motivate his workers, we have the perfect recipe for failure.

Why do workers leave their jobs?

The command "Do it because I say so because I sign your paychecks!" is being answered by many employees with "Not for long!" As I researched the reasons employees leave their jobs, I discovered that the majority don't leave their job, they leave their boss. Bad bosses are the problem.

75% of workers who voluntarily left their jobs did so because of their bosses and not the position itself.

Employees join companies but leave managers. A Gallup poll of more than 1 million employed U.S. workers concluded that the No. 1 reason people quit their jobs is a bad boss or immediate supervisor. 75% of workers who voluntarily left their jobs did so because of their bosses and not the position itself. Despite how good a job may be, people will quit if the reporting relationship is not healthy. *"People leave managers not companies...in the end, turnover is mostly a manager issue."*[4]

This book is principally written for Christian church members and church leaders, but the principles that apply to employment in the secular work force apply equally to volunteer organizations. The fact is, they apply with greater force because within the church, the paycheck is not a motivating factor. In all but the most legalistic churches the statement "you must do as I say because I am your pastor", is no longer credible. Christians change churches far more often than they change their jobs, and for far less serious leadership failures. For us who are in leadership in the local church this is kind of depressing, but it needn't be.

A new form of leadership

There is a new form of leadership arising within secular employment and the church. It does not rely on positional authority, in fact, it avoids it whenever possible. It is leadership through influence. It requires no title. It employs no threats. It is not manipulative. It sets people free to be themselves. It affirms and encourages their best attributes and abilities. It empowers people to be the best they can be.

In the local church, it empowers them to be all God designed them to be. It is not based on some innate gifting only available to a few. It can be learned. It has been hiding in plain sight for two thousand years. It is to be found in the Bible and its time has come.

> **There is a new form of leadership arising within secular employment and the church. It does not rely on positional authority, in fact, it avoids it whenever possible.**

There is a great irony existing today. The Christian church has had the power of influence available to it for two thousand years, yet the church has largely ignored it in favor of the ease of positional authority. Today many churches are led according to secular business principles, with the pastor as CEO.

Ironically, the secular business world has begun to explore non-positional leadership models. These models are exploring "servant leadership" and leadership through influence as the cutting edge of leadership development. It appears a role reversal is taking place, not just in leadership style, but in who is going to be most influential in leading the discussion. The church has the opportunity to drive the discussion. More than that, we can reclaim the power of influence within our church leadership and lead the discussion by example. It is time for the church's light to come out from under the bushel.

The remainder of this book will explore and contrast positional leadership with leadership through influence. Just to be clear, and at the risk of redundancy, let me say again; it would be a mistake to assume that I am arguing for replacing positional leadership with influence. There is a place for positional leadership in the church and society, but it is not the only way to lead and most of the time, it is not the best way to lead. As the old saying goes, "a place for everything and everything in its place." Let's begin with the place of positional leadership in the Bible, but first...

Some Questions to Consider:

1. Have you noticed a disrespect for authority in your culture? If so, is it increasing, decreasing, or "flat"?

2. Have you had any experience with a positional leader? If so, was it good or bad?

3. In the introduction to this book, I said that all of us can be a person of influence in some relationship. Do you agree? If so, with whom do you have influence?

4. Do you want your influence to grow?

Chapter 2: The Origin of Positional Authority

"And God said, 'Let there be light,' and there was light." Genesis 1:3

Positional authority has been with us since the moment of creation. "God said…" and it was! This is the ultimate act of positional authority. God merely speaks out loud and something non-existent comes into being. Kings need only to speak, and their words become facts. Positional authority has its beginning in God because He is the source of all that is, including authority. He is the first King, and He will be the last King. He is the eternal King. His authority will last forever.

Not only was God's positional authority active in creation, it is the means by which His creation [His Kingdom] is managed. What is important for our understanding of positional authority, is to realize that God has not chosen to manage His Kingdom directly. He has delegated His positional authority to mankind for the management of His kingdom. We see this first act of delegated positional authority in Genesis.

Then God said, "Let us make mankind in our image, in our likeness, so that <u>they may rule</u> over the fish in the sea and the birds in the sky, over the livestock and all the wild animals, and over all the creatures that move along the ground Gen. 1:26

Man's first act of delegated positional authority is of profound importance. God delegated the naming of all the animals to Adam. [Gen. 2:19-20] The significance of man naming the animals is found in the fact that, in the ancient near east, naming something was an act of dominion or authority over it. By allowing man to name the animals God was confirming His delegation of positional authority to mankind. What makes this act of delegated authority truly profound is that when Adam named all the animals it included the Snake! God gave Adam authority over Satan! From this moment, Satan's agenda became the removal of man from his place of delegated authority over him.

Picture this

To help tell the story we need to picture an image. Imagine that Adam is standing on a pedestal. It is the place of his positional authority. Imagine lines of authority coming down from God passing through Adam and going out to all of creation. Satan is off to the side below Adam, and he is subject to one of those lines of authority. He burns with jealously, pride and hatred for Adam and he longs to kick Adam off of his pedestal of positional authority.

It should be an easy task. Satan is much more powerful than Adam [a mere human]. Satan should be able to push Adam off the pedestal but for the fact that God's power, which is far greater than Satan's, protects God's delegated authority. In God's creation, authority trumps power. Mere power cannot displace Adam from his delegated positional authority. If Satan is going to displace Adam, he must use something other than force.

Adam has God's delegated positional authority for as long as he remains under it. While he remains on his pedestal he remains under God's authority, but should he choose to step out from under it, through disobedience, he will lose it. By using a lie, Satan tricked Adam into stepping sideways [disobedience] and Adam fell from the pedestal. Now he is no longer in a position of authority over evil. We call this "the fall" and that is exactly what it was – a fall from a position of delegated authority.

It is no coincidence that when Jesus came to restore the Kingdom of God one of His early acts was to return man's delegated positional authority to him, including his authority over evil. [Matthew 10:1, Mark 3:14-15, Luke 10:19]

Adam's sin did not thwart God's plan for reigning through delegated authority

Even though Adam failed to protect his delegated godly authority, God did not go to plan B. God continued to delegate His authority to imperfect people. Delegated authority remains God's plan A for the governance of His creation, for better or for worse.

Throughout the Old Testament God not only confirmed His delegation of positional authority but He allowed the redelegation of it. When Moses arrived at the promised land, he asked God to choose a leader to usher Israel into the promised land. God responded by telling Moses to "give him some of your authority" so that he might lead Israel. [Numbers 27:20]

Likewise, on the journey to the promised land Moses redelegated his authority to wise and respected men within the community, to have authority as commanders "of thousands, of hundreds, of fifties, and of tens and as tribal officials." [Deuteronomy 1:15-16]

In the New Testament Jesus brings with Him a new model of leadership and a new kind of authority, not in substitution of positional authority, but in addition to it.

It should be clear from these scriptures that positional authority was the model of leadership of the Old Testament. In the absence of the New Testament, it would be logical to conclude that positional authority is God's "default setting" for leadership in His present-day church. As we will see, the Old Testament is not the end of the

27

story. In the New Testament Jesus brings with Him a new model of leadership and a new kind of authority, not in substitution of positional authority, but in addition to it. The addition makes all the difference.

Before we introduce this new kind of authority, we need to explore positional authority as found in the Old Testament. The reason such an examination is important is because much of the defense of positional leadership in the church today is rooted in the positional leadership found in the Old Testament [for better, but usually for worse].

Old Testament positional leadership

Moses

Moses is the prototypical leader of the Old Testament. He was prophet, priest, and king [only in the sense of being God's governor over the people]. He is a "type" and foreshadowing of Jesus. [Deut. 18:15] He said one like me is coming and you must listen to Him. He is in effect saying, "one is coming who will lead like I do."

For this reason, we will examine the characteristics of Moses' positional leadership; how he came to lead and how he led.

A supernatural call to leadership

The first characteristic to note concerns the means through which God calls Moses into leadership. God reveals himself to Moses supernaturally. Moses encounters a flaming bush that will not burn up. Even more supernatural, the voice of God speaks to him from the bush! Here is overwhelming evidence for Moses to believe that he is hearing the genuine voice of God. One would think that such an experience would fill Moses with the faith necessary to agree to taking the leadership role God is about to call him to. Not so!

God tells Moses to go back to Egypt to confront Pharaoh and then to lead the people of Israel out of Egypt. What God is offering Moses is a place in history on par with Abraham's, but Moses doesn't want the honor because he does not see himself as qualified. [Exodus 3:11] God's response is to perform the "staff to snake and back again miracle." Still Moses argues that he is a terrible public speaker, and that God should find someone else. God suggests Aaron as Moses' public relations agent and so Moses, having run out of excuses, agrees to become the foremost leader of the Old Testament.

Not seeking a position of leadership

The second and most important characteristic of Moses positional leadership is that he does not seek it, in fact, he tries to avoid it. Herein lies one of the secrets to successful positional leadership. Those who want it least are the ones who are usually not corrupted by it.

A conversational relationship with God

The third characteristic of Moses' positional leadership is that it is relational. Moses begins a conversational relationship with God from the first moment, and it lasts throughout his entire leadership career. The importance of a positional leader being in an intimate relationship with God cannot be overstated. It is this relationship that keeps the leader safe, both for his own spiritual survival and for the good of

> The importance of a positional leader being in an intimate relationship with God cannot be overstated. It is this relationship that keeps the leader safe, both for his own spiritual survival and for the good of those he leads.

those he leads. As we examine positional leadership throughout the Old Testament, we will see this truth confirmed again and again.

Joshua

Joshua was God's choice to succeed Moses. Joshua's call into positional leadership contains the same three characteristics as Moses'. Joshua was a witness to all the supernatural miracles God performed through Moses while Israel crossed the desert to the promised land. He also led the attack against Jericho in which God reduced the mighty walls of the city to rubble while the warriors of Israel did nothing but worship. That's supernatural!

Like Moses, Joshua did not attempt to assume leadership, he merely responded to the voice of God. He did not covet a leadership role, God thrust it upon him.

Like Moses, he too had a conversational relationship with God. More than 17 times in the book of Joshua we find God and Joshua in conversation.

Gideon

After the nation of Israel entered the promised land [Canaan] we find a period of national decline. God gave very specific instruction about remaining separate, both religiously and socially, from the pagan cultures and inhabitants of the conquered land. Despite this fact, Israel ignored His commands and adopted the idolatry of the false religions surrounding it. As well, Israel engaged in the forbidden practice of intermarriage, which further angered God. God's response was swift; He withdrew His hand of protection. Calamity and suffering followed for Israel in the form of subservience to the very nations they had just conquered.

This period of Israel's history is referred to as the time of the "Judges." The period was characterized by Israel's apostasy, leading to subservience, leading to desperation, leading to God's deliverance through judges. These judges were raised up by God as military leaders to go to war to liberate Israel. Soon after God's liberation, the nation would again forget God's commands and the cycle of decline and deliverance would begin again.

During this period, Israel's success depended on the leadership qualities of the judges. Sadly, for every good judge there seemed to soon follow a bad one, or a series of bad ones. Interestingly, the period of the judges, both for good and bad, is summed up by two judges: Gideon and his son Abimelech. Gideon is our example of a good judge.

Gideon began his tenure as a judge as did Moses, with a supernatural encounter. An angel of the Lord came to visit Gideon with a command to go and save Israel. The encounter is very similar to that between Moses and God. [Judges 6:14-16]

Like Moses, Gideon believed himself unqualified for the leadership position God was calling him to. Like Moses, Gideon required a supernatural sign, two in fact, to convince him of the wisdom of God's call. [Judges 6:36-40] Gideon had no ambition driving him to seek leadership, it was thrust upon him. After delivering Israel from oppression the nation of Israel asked for Gideon and his lineage to rule over them. Gideon refused. [Judges 6:22-23]

Gideon, as well, had a conversational relationship with God. The story of Gideon's leadership is the working out of his conversations with God.

The story of Gideon's leadership does not end well. "No sooner had Gideon died" than the nation slid into the worship of false gods and idols. [Judges 8:33-34]

This is the pattern to be found in the story of positional leadership throughout the Old Testament. The spiritual health of the nation depends on the spiritual health of its leader. The writer of Judges emphasizes this fact with the use of the phrase "no sooner."

This pattern of rapid decay, following the passing of a godly leader, begs some very important questions. How can this happen so quickly? How can people being blessed by God turn from Him so thoroughly and so quickly? What was going on within their hearts during the time they were "worshipping Him"? After we have finished our survey of positional leadership in the Old Testament, we will return to these questions because the answer to these questions is the foundation for the model of leadership found in the New Testament. The answer is worth the wait.

Abimelech

To the degree Gideon's leadership was godly, his son Abimelech's was evil. He convinced his 69 brothers to let him rule over Israel and after they made their decision public, he had all but one of them killed! We should note that Abimelech assumed that God had no choice in who was to follow Gideon's leadership. He assumed that the succession common to the pagan cultures surrounding Israel should apply to Israel. This is a clear break from God's methodology.

Israel suffered under Abimelech's rule. Abimelech set fire to a temple in which approximately 1000 men and women [probably including children] were hiding. They were all burned to death.

Fortunately for our sense of justice, "what goes around comes around" for Abimelech. While attempting to set another fire to a tower to destroy those who would not bow to him, a woman dropped a mill stone from the top of the tower. Her aim was perfect; the mill stone landed on his head. Being a misogynist, rather than admit that a woman had struck him a mortal blow, he had his armor bearer kill him with a sword. [Judges 9:50-56]

The remainder of the book of Judges repeats the same story; a good leader followed by a string of bad leaders. A nation continually slipping from honoring God to quickly dishonoring Him, all depending upon the spiritual state of the leader.

The book of Judges reveals Israel's error in coveting a king. Too much power in the hands of a leader who neither knows God nor was chosen by Him is always a recipe for disaster. More than that, the institution of kingship was never God's plan for leading His people. In the next chapter this becomes apparent as we examine the prophet Samuel and his leadership role in the nation of Israel.

Summary Points:

The Old Testament provides us with three safeguards to the abuse of positional authority. They are:

1. A supernatural call to leadership,
2. A lack of desire for the position, and
3. A "conversational" relationship with God throughout the duration of that leadership.

This is certainly what categorized successful positional leadership in the Old Testament, but does that necessarily mean these principles apply today? As well, if the answer is yes, what do we mean by a supernatural call to leadership today? Should we be looking for a burning bush? And what do we mean by a "conversational" relationship with God? Is that even possible today? These are very important questions, so let's try to answer them in their order:

1. Regarding a supernatural call to leadership:

"A number of years ago a denomination I was familiar with did a survey of all their church plants – both those that succeeded and those that failed. They tested for a variety of factors believed to be important to a successful church plant. These included adequate startup funding, level of theological education of the pastor, training for the startup leadership team, demographic studies of the proposed region, etc. One of the questions asked was, "Did you hear God tell you to do this church plant?"

As it turns out, approximately 90% of those who succeeded "heard" God tell them to do the plant. Conversely, approximately 90% of those who failed said they did not "hear" God tell them to do the plant. All of the other factors were inconclusive"[5].

Hearing God imparts faith. Planting a successful church is fraught with difficulties and doubts, sufficient to cause many leaders to close the doors and walk away. After all, if you are not sure God called you to do something then it is easy to quit when circumstances suggest it would be wise to do so. Hearing God's voice may be the key to perseverance. So, how does God "speak" in such a way that we can be certain we have heard from Him? Does it have to be a "burning bush" experience?

An experience is "supernatural" when it cannot be adequately explained naturally. A series of extremely unlikely coincidences can result in a certainty that God is communicating with us. A stranger walking up to you on the street and telling you what you wrote in your prayer journal that morning and what God wants to say to you about it would probably qualify. For more examples of this kind of guidance you might enjoy reading our book, Reluctantly Supernatural in an Age of Reason.[6]

2. A lack of desire for the position:

Very little needs to be said on this point. Unless someone is feigning reluctance in order to deceive, it is easy to spot a reluctance to lead when it arises. God called my friend Robert to pastor a prestigious mega church in a very desirable city. The problem was he did not want the job. He wrestled with God for three months until this conversation settled the matter:

Robert: I am not primarily an administrator!

God: We'll work on that.

Robert: I take things too personally and get my feelings hurt!

God: We'll toughen you up.

Robert: But there are plenty of others who really want the position!

God: I want you.

Robert: Me? Are you sure?

God: I am calling you. I will be with you.

Robert: OK, but to be clear, I am open to something else...

God: Trust me!

Robert took the job and led the church for many years, seeing it grow in size and influence. Robert's interaction with God illustrates our next point.

3. Having a conversational relationship with God:

My understanding of the Bible, and my experience, lead me to believe that our God desires to communicate with His children in a direct way – heart to heart and mind to mind. He places His thoughts in our minds, both for ourselves and for others. He is doing this far more often than we may notice. Our failure to notice His "voice" is because we are often so distracted by the pace of our modern lives that we fail to hear His "still small voice." Sadly, for many of us who are in leadership in His church, we are so distracted by working **for** Him that we miss being **with** Him.

To survive the temptations that come with positional leadership we need to hear God's voice regularly. This means carving out and protecting a daily time to slow down, be still, and simply listen for His thoughts.

For an expanded study of the characters and principles found in this chapter, including expanded scripture references, please refer to Appendix 1. on page 251.

Now on to Samuel and the Kings. Sounds like a rock band doesn't it. But first...

Some Questions to Consider:

1. Can you list the three characteristics of leadership found in the lives of Moses, Joshua, & Gideon?

2. Can you explain why each of them is essential to successful positional leadership?

3. Why was it so easy for the nation of Israel to turn away from God "as soon as" a godly leader died?

4. How often does God communicate with you?

Chapter 3: Samuel and the Kings

When we think of Samuel, we tend to remember him as a prophet of God. He clearly heard and spoke for God, but he was much more than that. God chose Samuel as the leader of the nation. Like Moses, he acted as prophet, priest and governor. He occupied these three roles until God acquiesced to Israel's reprehensible demand for a king. Samuel had the same three characteristics illustrated in Moses' call to leadership:

1. It came as a result of supernatural encounters with God. [1 Samuel 1:15-22]
2. He did not seek leadership.
3. Samuel as well, had a conversational relationship with God.

Samuel's role as Israel's leader ended when he appointed his two sons as judges to lead the nation. They did not follow his example of godliness. They pursued **"dishonest gain and accepted bribes and perverted justice."** [1 Samuel 8:1-3] Because of their abuse of their position of authority, the people of Israel lobbied Samuel to appoint a king over them. They specifically demanded a king **"such as all the other nations have."** [1 Samuel 8:5]

It is important to note that by asking for such a king they were asking for a leader without accountability to any authority, including God Himself. They were lobbying for a positional leader who would hold absolute authority and power.

Samuel took the people's demand for a king to God, and God's response was somewhat confusing. He made it perfectly clear that Israel's demand for a king was a rejection of His rule over them, but He told Samuel to accede to the people's demand. God commanded Samuel to warn the people as to what life under a king would be like. Here is a summary of God's description of what the people should expect of life under a king. [1 Samuel 8:10-18]

1. He will conscript your sons and force them to serve as foot soldiers to run in front of His chariots [the first to die].
2. He will put them to work serving him and his army.
3. He will take your daughters and force them to serve him.
4. He will take the best of your fields, vineyards, and olive groves and give them to his attendants.
5. He will take your servants from you, as well as the best of your cattle and donkeys.
6. He will take you as slaves and when that happens you will cry out for deliverance from God, but He will not help you.

It is very important to understand that God was not opposed to any particular choice of who would be king, He was opposed to the institution of kingship. It was not His plan for Israel to be ruled by any king. He was to be Israel's King.

It is hard to imagine how God's warning to Israel could have been any clearer, yet even after the warning, the people demanded a king. [1 Samuel 8:19-20]

God instructed Samuel to give Israel what it wanted even when He knew the disaster it would lead to. This begs the question "why?"

All of these dire consequences came to pass due to the abuse of positional authority.

It appears that God is not interested in exercising His positional authority without regard for our choices, even when those choices are not in our best interests. Although God has perfect positional authority [He is the King of

God is not interested in exercising His positional authority without regard for our choices, even when those

- -   -

Kings] He regularly chooses to lead us in a more indirect way, in many cases through trial and error. **He allows the freedom He has given us to be the means of our instruction.** Throughout the Old Testament He repeatedly allowed Israel to make her own bad choices and to live with the consequences. Israel learned to accept Him as King the hard way and only for short periods of time.

Learning in the school of hard knocks

I have been a pastor a long time and I have noticed something about human nature. There are two kinds of people; those who learn by listening to wise counsel and those who reject wise counsel and learn through their mistakes. In my experience the latter are in the overwhelming majority. There is something about our pride that tells us that we will be the exception to the rule. "Most people may need wise counsel, but I am smart enough and strong enough and capable enough to do this without God's help." Famous last words.

God has the patience to allow us to learn the hard way, but perhaps it is even deeper than that. Perhaps He doesn't want us to obey Him because we have to, but because we want to. Could it be that He wants our hearts and not just our obedience?

As a good father, God knows that if He forces us to obey, our motive for obedience becomes fear.

It is hugely important to remember that of all the titles that He could have used to describe His relationship with His people, particularly in the New Testament, He chose "Father." He is indeed the perfect father. As a good father, God knows that if He forces us to obey, our motive for obedience becomes fear. As a perfect loving father, He wants to be loved even more than feared. This means that His leadership will have to be something other than purely positional. More on this later...

The Kings

We don't need to do a detailed examination of the Kings because this period mirrors, on a larger scale, the leadership principles found during the period of the judges. What we find is a history of good and bad kings which corresponds with times of prosperity and blessing, followed by times of decay and oppression. There are a few kings we should look at in some detail. They are Saul, David, and Absalom.

Saul

Saul was the first king of Israel. Although God did not want Israel led by a king, He acquiesced to the people's requests and gave them a king. Saul was God's choice of king for the purpose of delivering Israel from the Philistines.

Like Moses, Saul's call into leadership was supernatural – it was the result of a very accurate prophetic word which was confirmed the day after it was received. [1 Sam.9:15-16]

> If Saul had had a direct conversational relationship with God, he probably would have been able to overcome his fear of man and end his reign successfully.

Like Moses, Saul did not seek a position of leadership. Like Moses, he was reluctant to accept the position of King. [1 Sam. 9:17-10:2 & 1 Sam. 10:21-22]

Although Saul conformed to two of the three characteristics of God-ordained leaders, he failed in the third. Saul had no direct relationship with God. The prophet Samuel was the intermediary between God and Saul. As Saul's confidence grew, his obedience to God's word through Samuel waned. Eventually, Saul's disobedience to the word of the Lord through Samuel disqualified his lineage from succeeding him as king.

Because of his insecurity and fear of man, Saul ended his reign in tragedy. It is fair to reach the conclusion that if Saul had had a direct conversational relationship with God, he probably would have been able to overcome his fear of man and end his reign successfully. Sadly, for Saul's lineage, God chose a man after His own heart as the king upon which God would build a lasting dynasty.

David

While Saul was still King, God told Samuel to anoint the next King of Israel. God gave Samuel specific instructions as to where to find His next king, but He did not tell him who it would be. When the family of the candidates was brought to Samuel he assumed, based on the fine appearance of one of the sons, who the next king would be. God corrected Samuel saying,

"Do not consider his appearance or his height, for I have rejected him. The Lord does not look at the things man looks at. Man looks at the outward appearance, but the Lord looks at the heart." [1 Sam. 16:6-7]

This is a hugely important statement because it reveals God's most important criteria for leadership. Whereas we often look at talents and abilities or even physical appearance, God looks at character.

Samuel saw all the candidate sons and none of them were God's choice. The youngest son had been overlooked because he was out in the field working. He was too young to be considered. He was David, described as a man after God's own heart. When he was brought to Samuel, God confirmed David as the future king and Samuel anointed him. This confirmation was supernatural in that it was directed through a prophetic word. As further supernatural confirmation of his call, from the moment of his anointing the Spirit of the Lord came upon David "in power."

Even though David knew he was to be king, he never coveted the throne. It would be many years before David assumed the throne as Israel's King and the intervening years would test David's character to the extreme.

Patience and self-control

His first test involved patience. What must it have been like to know you are God's choice for King, yet you start your training by playing your harp for your demonized king, who expresses his thanks by trying to kill you? [1 Sam. 18:10-11]

Humility

The second test involved humility. After killing the Philistine giant Goliath, David continued to win battles against Israel's enemies. The common people sang songs about him singing, **"Saul has slain his thousands, and David his tens of thousands."** [1 Sam. 18:6-7]

Despite the adulation of the people, it never affected David's loyalty to Saul, yet Saul became very jealous of David. In an attempt to ensnare David, Saul offered David his daughter Merab in marriage. David refused by saying, **"Who am I, and what is my family or my father's clan in Israel, that I should become the king's son-in-law?"** [1 Sam. 18:18] He never sought the Kingship. He sounds a lot like Gideon, doesn't he?

Submission and loyalty

The third test involved loyalty to David's persecutor. Despite David's complete loyalty to Saul, Saul's jealously of David's popularity mutated into hatred. Saul decided to kill David. David fled Saul's court and lived for more than a year running from Saul's army.

David refused to harm Saul even though the circumstances were available to do so. He had a perfect opportunity to kill Saul, but he refused to. He could easily have justified killing Saul by the circumstantial evidence that God had delivered Saul into his hands – a logical conclusion made and urged by David's men. Despite a golden opportunity to kill Saul and take the throne, David reaffirmed his loyalty to King Saul even though Saul had come to kill him.

After a bloody fight between the houses of Saul and David, David was declared King of both Judah and Israel. He reigned for 40 years, and his reign is the highwater mark for kingship in the Old Testament. During his reign he defeated all of Israel's enemies which included taking Jerusalem from the Jebusites. He also returned the Ark of the Lord to Jerusalem.

David can be described as the "warrior king." He was at his best when at war. Under his military command the nation of Israel grew in territory, power and prestige. Sadly, the same success cannot be claimed for his peace-time rule.

It is probably not a coincidence that David's first failure as a monarch came when he chose not to accompany his army into battle. [2 Sam. 11:1] While at home on the roof of his palace he saw Bathsheba bathing. She was the wife of one of his most loyal soldiers. He had her brought to him and he slept with her. When he found out that she was pregnant with his child, he tried to deflect responsibility from himself by calling her husband Uriah home to sleep with her in the hopes of having Uriah believe the child was his.

Out of loyalty to his fellow soldiers, Uriah refused to enjoy his wife while his fellows were on the battlefield risking their lives. David tried twice to trick Uriah into sleeping with his wife, but Uriah refused to do so. As a final solution, David had Uriah sent into a fierce battle in which the commander had been ordered by David to abandon Uriah and assure his death. The plan worked. David was now guilty of adultery **and** murder.

Openness to criticism

To David's credit, when he was confronted with his sin by Nathan the prophet, he sincerely repented, but not before Nathan prophesied God's punishment – a future of violence within David's household and the death of the baby born from his adultery. [2 Sam. 12:7-12] David's son Absalom fulfilled Nathan's prophecy.

If we look back at our summary of bad Old Testament leaders thus far there is little doubt Abimelech is at the top of the garbage heap...until we meet Absalom.

Absalom

Abimelech did his father the honor of waiting until his death to seize leadership. Not so with Absalom. Absalom worked tirelessly behind his father's back to marshal a rebellion against King David. The rebellion would probably have succeeded but for a tip from a messenger that allowed David and his court to flee Jerusalem. David left ten of his concubines behind to care for his palace. During Absalom's coupe, he slept with all ten of David's wives in the sight of all the people. [2 Sam. 16:22] It is hard to imagine a more disrespectful act toward one's father.

David ruled long enough to die of natural causes, somewhat surprising given the bloodshed that characterized his reign. He was indeed a warrior king, yet he conformed to the Mosaic model of positional leadership by having a conversational relationship with God. [1 Sam. 23:1-4, Sam. 23:10-12, 2 Sam. 21:1-2

We could continue with our study of the Kings of the Old Testament but what we would find is just more of what we

44

have already observed. The History of the Kings is a sadly predictable pattern of short periods of obedient godly Kings framed by much longer periods of corrupt and evil kings, bringing ruin upon the nation. The rule is, apostasy followed by short periods of revival and blessing, all dependent upon the ungodly or godly character of the positional leader.

We are now able to draw some conclusions about positional leadership in the Old Testament, so let's do it. But first...

Some Questions to Consider:

1. Gideon, Samuel, & David were all godly leaders, but their sons   were the opposite. What do you think went wrong?

2. What do you think it takes to avoid being corrupted by positional leadership?

3. God's pattern for choosing a leader is threefold: 1. Make His call to leadership supernatural, 2. Choose a person who does not covet the position, 3. Choose someone who will seek an intimate relationship of communication with Him. Why are each of these important?

4. Why do you think the nation of Israel wanted a King?

Chapter 4: The Good and the Bad of "The Boss"

"Meet the new boss. Same as the old boss."
Won't Get Fooled Again, Pete Townshend, The Who

This lyric pretty much sums up the history of the Kings of Israel. If following God is the criterion for defining a good king, then there were only 5 good kings. There were 33 who did not follow God. This disappointing ratio should not come as a surprise given the warning God gave Israel in response to its demand for a king. All the dire consequences God warned of came to pass as a result of Israel being led by a king. This fact alone should have us questioning the institution of Kingship [and unfettered positional authority], but the more relevant question is "why?" Why is Kingship almost always destructive?

I believe the answer has to do with the nature of positional leadership. To be a king is to have the ultimate position of power. It is the zenith of positional leadership. In contemporary terms, it is to be a dictator. As far as the relationship between king and subject is concerned, the authority of a king is absolute. Given human nature, this must facilitate abuse.

The abuses of positional leadership

Here are some of the abuses we should note from our brief survey of positional leadership in the Old Testament:

1. Unfettered Power.

Kings, by definition, are not responsible to any human authority. Where there exists no requirement for a positional leader to be accountable to any human authority, the leader has no governing influence operating to check his or her basest instincts. It is trite to quote Lord Acton's famous observation "Power corrupts, and absolute power corrupts absolutely" but history has proven his assertion that "a person's sense of morality lessens as his or her power increases" [Lord Acton, British historian of the late nineteenth and early twentieth centuries.]

Some readers may be too young to remember the tragedy of the Jonestown Massacre. Nine hundred members of an American cult called the Peoples' Temple died in a mass suicide/murder under the direction of their leader Jim Jones. It provides a sadly perfect example of positional leadership gone horribly wrong – families held captive against their will, forced to drink poisoned Kool-Aid.

Who corrects a king?

Where human critics are absent or shunned, the only accountability possible for a king is God. This explains why a conversational relationship with God is so essential to a positional leader. Where it is absent, it is all too easy to dismiss the counsel of those persons God has placed in the leader's life.

Saul provides an excellent example of this syndrome. Saul had unfettered authority to rule as he saw fit. As a counterbalance to this, God gave him Samuel as a prophet and Jonathan as his most trusted son and counselor. Saul had more than enough proof from his own experience to know with certainty that Samuel spoke accurately for God. Despite this evidence Saul refused to obey Samuel's clear instructions regarding waiting for Samuel to minister to the Lord before a critical battle. Saul's disobedience cost his lineage the kingdom!

Twice, when Saul pursued David to kill him, Jonathan reasoned with his father to present the case for David's obvious loyalty to Saul. Saul ceased his pursuit of David momentarily, but soon returned to his fear-driven, irrational attacks. Saul was a leader who could not be corrected by those God had given him for that purpose, and as such he was living outside of God's control as well. Unfettered authority is a powerful temptation to complete self-will. Few can resist it!

David is one of those who could resist it, for most of his life. David had two sources of accountability in his life against unfettered authority and complete self-will: Nathan the prophet and David's own conversational relationship with God.

It is more than arguable that David's sin was worse than Saul's. Saul disobeyed God's prophet and tried to kill a faithful servant. David succeeded in killing his faithful servant after committing adultery with his wife! On top of that he did it deceitfully. Saul lost his lineage of kingship and David did not. Why? The simplest answer is that David chose to repent, but the means of David's conviction of sin is what truly differentiates the two.

David was confronted by Nathan the prophet, who used a clever story to reveal David's sin to him. David **listened** to the prophet, took his words to heart, and wholeheartedly repented. David listened to the voice of God through his counselor and Saul did not. David **welcomed accountability** and Saul refused it.

At the risk of redundancy, positional authority without human accountability is dangerous for both the leader and his followers.

God's prototype for a positional leader was Moses; someone who combines three functions: 1. Someone who speaks to God for the people [priest], 2. Someone who speaks to the people for God [prophet] and 3. Someone who administers God's laws over the people [governor, judge, king.] The first two functions require a conversational relationship with God. Arguably, so does the third.

48

The institution of kingship, as found in the pagan cultures surrounding Israel, was inconsistent with God's three-functioned model of leadership. It only came close on the third function, that of governing. Without direct communication with God a positional leader governs in the absence of divine wisdom.

The history of the Kings of Israel is largely one of animosity between the prophets and the kings, the priests and the kings, and occasionally the prophets and the priests. This disunity between the kings and their God-ordained counselors provides a headstrong leader with further justification for extreme self-will.

"They are always differing with me! They are making my leadership difficult! There's no point in trying to listen to them! They are just slowing me down! They are just being critical! I am going to ignore them! And if I can't ignore them, I'll just find a way around them!"

I wonder how many senior pastors have had these thoughts about their boards of elders.

Positional leadership promotes and facilitates the dismissal of good advice. Business professor James O'Toole has added that,

"as one's power grows, one's willingness to listen shrinks..."[7]

2. Positional leadership is a good place to hide.

Because positional leadership can dismiss wise counsel easily, it becomes the perfect place to hide from personal blind spots, weaknesses, character flaws, and sin.

Because positional leadership can dismiss wise counsel easily, it becomes the perfect place to hide from personal blind spots, weaknesses, character flaws, and sin. Saul is a perfect example

49

of this problem. Saul was an inherently insecure man. He was afraid of failure. On the day of his anointing as king, Saul was hiding in the baggage. He was afraid to be king.

Saul had a deep fear of man. Samuel prophesied to Saul that he was to **completely** destroy the Amalekites and **everything** that belonged to them. After the battle Samuel discovered that Saul had disobeyed God's instructions to destroy all the possessions of the Amalekites. Saul had spared some of the cattle to use as sacrifices. When confronted by Samuel, Saul said,

"I have sinned. I violated the Lord's command and your instructions. I was afraid of the people and so I gave in to them." [1 Sam. 15:24]

Saul suffered from a deep insecurity and fear of man. Saul's position of king made it possible for him to hide from his deepest fears because there was no one to confront him with them. Leading from fear and insecurity usually guarantees poor decision making. Saul's refusal to face his fears cost him the future promises of the kingdom.

Although positional leadership offers the insecure a perfect place to hide, it does not mean that every positional leader will use it to hide from fear. David lived with fear for years as he ran from Saul's army. A quick read through the Psalms will reveal the deepest fears of David's heart. The difference between Saul hiding his fears behind his position and David dealing with them is the fact of the Psalms themselves. David did the opposite of Saul.

Saul hid his fears, but David sang his fears to his men! He made his fears public! Not just for the period of his life on the run, but for all his life and all of church history! David turned his fears into worship! It is important to note that what made it possible for David to do this was his conversational relationship with God. Before he sang his fears to his men, he sang them to God.

What we are discussing here can be referred to as "self-awareness."

David had it and Saul didn't.

Self-awareness

Self-awareness is comprised of two distinct understandings. The first is internal. The question is, "Am I aware of my own inner issues; my fears, hopes, anxieties, strengths, weaknesses, temperament, sins, etc.?" The second is external. The question here is, "Am I accurately aware of how others see me with respect to these same issues?"

Self -awareness is hugely important to successful leadership. Tasha Eurich, organizational psychologist writes:

> *"We've found that internal self-awareness is associated with higher job and relationship satisfaction, personal and social control, and happiness; it is negatively related to anxiety, stress, and depression.*
>
> *For leaders who see themselves as their employees do, [external self-awareness] their employees tend to have a better relationship with them, feel more satisfied with them, and see them as more effective in general."*[8]

Eurich's research revealed that being internally self-aware does not lead to being externally self-aware, in fact there is no correlation between the two. The reason this is important is because the more powerful the leadership position the less likely the leader is to be internally **and** externally self-aware.

With power comes pride. Eurich found that the greater the power held by the leader, the greater they overestimated their skills and abilities. She concluded that this is because the more senior the leader, the fewer there are above them to provide honest feedback. As for those below them, few will risk endangering their careers by bringing constructive feedback to their boss. She cites business professor James O'Toole who adds "that as one's power grows, one's willingness to listen shrinks, either because they think they know more than their employees or because seeking feedback will come at a cost."[9]

For positional leaders, the likelihood of high internal self-awareness together with high external self-awareness is very low. This is a recipe for "bad boss of the year" and is a destroyer of influence. We will look at self-awareness in more detail later.

3. Positional leadership provides false, yet instantaneous, self-worth and so attracts the insecure.

One of the advantages of being in church leadership for many years is the opportunity to observe people, especially those who seek to be leaders. One of the people I observed seeking leadership was myself. In the early bloom of my decision to make Jesus the Lord of my life I found myself drawn to becoming a leader. Because I had a genuine love for God, I believed that my motives for seeking leadership were entirely pure. And so, the self-deception began. The truth of the matter was that I grew up with a mother who suffered from depression. As a child she was in and out of the psych ward during my formative years. Unknown to me, I grew up with a deep fear of being abandoned by my primary source of security.

I was able to bury my fear because I was smart, talented and could achieve the security I craved by being liked and necessary to people. This made the pastorate the perfect place for me to exercise my denial and self-deception. I led from a need to be needed. I lived under the fear of man. The harder I worked to love people, the more I saw myself as "spiritual" and "Christlike." The problem was that I was afraid to exercise any form of tough love for fear of being rejected. What a mess!

The story of my healing comes in another book. My point in sharing my mess is that most of the time a leader's motives for seeking leadership are mixed. Not just mixed; but often hidden from himself and others. This fact highlights the need for internal self-awareness.

> **Positional leadership often attracts those who seek a title rather than a responsibility. A title always provides an instant affirmation of worth.**

Over the years I have watched potential leaders seeking positional leadership for the wrong reasons. One of the signs of motivation coming from insecurity is the insistence on having a position with an impressive title. Positional leadership often attracts those who seek a title rather than a responsibility. A title always provides an instant affirmation of worth. I have seen leaders, apparently committed to growing in leadership responsibility, working hard without the recognition a title provides who, shortly after the title was given, began to shirk the responsibility they once shouldered. The temptation is to expend effort to improve the appearance of success rather than expending it to make the right choices to ensure success.

Far too often we view titles as badges of honor rather than descriptions of function. Titles are valuable when their purpose is to describe who is responsible for what in an organization. When they are valued as honorifics to be possessed and displayed, they are nothing more than accessories to our pride.

The one thing no church needs to promote within its leadership is pride.

Titles appeal to either of two leadership failings; insecurity or pride. Both failings result in a leader who takes every opportunity to remind those around him of his title:

"As your senior pastor, I need to tell you this...."

"As chairman of the elders board I want to make clear that..."

"I hope you appreciate receiving this personal phone call from your worship pastor..."

As the youth pastor it is my duty to tell you about what your son did on Friday night..."

These statements say more about the person making the statement than about the statement itself. They are subtly saying either "listen to me because I am insecure" or "listen to me because I am an important person." In both cases the use of the title is undermining their credibility as anything more than a poor positional leader.

4. Unfettered Positional Leadership Promotes a Sycophant Culture.

Although we have already touched on this syndrome it bears further exploration. When a leader is not accountable to any authority within the immediate organization, he or she quickly attracts "yes men" and sycophants. No employee or volunteer who values her job will risk confronting her boss with his shortcomings more than once. Where the boss refuses to entertain the confrontation, the worker soon realizes, "If I want to keep my job, I must never do this again!" And so, a culture of sycophants is developed.

In a very interesting article entitled, "Why Leaders Lose Their Way"[10] Bill George quoted Senator John Ensign's farewell speech to his fellow senators. Senator Ensign was resigning because he covered up an extramarital affair with monetary payoffs. Here is a portion of his farewell speech:

"When one takes a position of leadership, there is a very real danger of getting caught up in the hype surrounding that status ... Surround yourselves with people who will be honest with you about how you really are and what you are becoming, and then make them promise to not hold back... from telling you the truth."

When a leader has wise counselors but refuses to listen to them, they soon have nothing to say. They reason accurately, "why risk my job when he is not going to listen anyway?"

"Leaders who don't listen will eventually be surrounded by people who have nothing to say." Andy Stanley

Leaders who do not have wise counselors to bring constructive criticism risk operating in the dark regarding the culture they are creating. This can happen without any callous or indifferent intention. Here is a good example of how it can happen. I will paraphrase an article from Business Week.[11]

An internal review of Dell Inc.'s subordinate management found Michael Dell to be impersonal and detached. It found the president Kevin Rollins to be autocratic and antagonistic. A further survey found that half of the company's employees would leave if they got the chance. In a genuine display of humility and vulnerability, both Dell and Rollins took personal responsibility to correct their external self-awareness. Without delay Dell spoke to his top managers and admitted that he is a hugely shy person who sometimes reacts by being aloof or unapproachable. He promised to become a more accessible and personal leader. As a follow-up, a video tape of his self-revelation was shown to every manager in the company, several thousand!

Dell and Rollins then took it a step further; Dell kept a model bulldozer on his desk to remind him to listen to his managers without "bulldozing" them, and Rollins got a Curious George doll to remind him to listen to his advisors before making major decisions.

This story reinforces the conclusion that a willingness to listen, together with a willingness to receive correction and change, results in loyal employees and employers who acquire greater influence. It is also an exercise in humility, which will be discussed later in this book.

5. Positional leadership is Good for War and Bad for Peace.

The vast majority of positional leaders found in the Old Testament were in leadership to make war. They were either fighting to take territory or fighting to defend it. A battle is never fought by committee. Decisions must be made quickly, often on a moment's notice. A hierarchy of chain of command is essential to success. The same can be said for any emergency. In an emergency someone must take charge and issue orders which must be obeyed without question.

In emergencies, and in war, the best interest of the people is met by a take charge, decisive, authoritarian leader. The same cannot be said for peacetime. In times of peace the people generally suffer when led by such a leader. Beyond the warnings given by God, which describe what life will be like living under a king, the people suffer even when the king makes perfect decisions. This is because being led by an all-

Being led by an all-powerful, authoritative leader disallows those led the opportunity to make their own decisions. This stunts their growth into mature adults.

56

powerful, authoritative leader disallows those led the opportunity to make their own decisions. This stunts their growth into mature adults. Allow an old man an example from the 1970s. In the 70s a movement began in the U.S. which became known as the "Shepherding Movement." I remember talking to a friend I had not seen for several years who had become a part of the movement.

He described living in a communal house in which the leader made all the decisions for all those living in the house. I became alarmed when he told me the leader decided who would date whom. I became truly frightened when he told me that the leaders routinely decided who should marry whom. As far as my friend was concerned this "shepherding" of the flock was a safeguard against immaturity. As it turned out, many people were badly hurt within the movement. The movement fell into disrepute and dissolved. There is a glaring irony in this example.

The irony is that the movement actually facilitated immaturity. It did this by moving the responsibility for good decision making from the sheep to the shepherds. As I have already mentioned, most of us learn our best lessons through trial and error. We learn as much from our bad choices as our good ones, often more. The more positional the leadership, the less responsibility and opportunity to grow for those being led.

Not only is the decision making of the people affected, but the positional leadership also found in the Old Testament came between the people and their own relationship with God. This result is so important that it requires its own chapter, but first one more related and unfortunate consequence of positional leadership.

6. The Positional Leader's relationship with God becomes the "God Experience" of the People.

As we have already seen, when a godly king rules, the people experience God's blessing. They are riding on the spiritual coattails of their king. Conversely, when the king is ungodly, the people suffer, often more than the king. This is because the people do not have their own relationship with God. Their experience of God is a consequence of their leader's relationship with God. This explains how Israel could go so wrong so fast after the death of a godly king when he was replaced by an ungodly one.

A leader who does not promote an independent relationship with God within his flock encourages his congregation to see God through the lens of his relationship with God.

The same thing happens in legalistic churches led by authoritarian leaders. The people often live their relationship with God vicariously through their leader. A leader who does not promote independent relationships with God within his flock encourages his congregation to see God through the lens of his relationship with God. Of course, this is really no relationship with God at all, it is merely spiritual voyeurism.

Some Questions to Consider:

1. How is unfettered authority or power corrupting?

2. Positional Leadership is a good place to hide from our blind spots, weaknesses and insecurities. Why?

3. What do you understand internal and external self-awareness to be? Why are they important?

4. Why does Positional Leadership attract the insecure leader?

5. What attracts leaders to titles?

6. Have you had an experience with a Positional Leader in your life? Was it good or bad? Why?

Chapter 5: The Institutionalization of External Control

"I Faught the Law and the Law Won"
Bobby Fuller Four, 1966

"When the people saw the thunder and lightning and heard the trumpet and saw the mountain in smoke, they trembled with fear. They stayed at a distance and said to Moses, 'Speak to us yourself and we will listen. But do not have God speak to us or we will die.'" Exodus 20:18-19

This short dialogue between the people of Israel and Moses is one of the saddest conversations in the Bible. Sad because it is the moment in which the nation of Israel rejected a "conversational relationship" with God. As we will see it is also the moment when positional leadership became institutionalized within a legal system. This moment is so important it bears close examination, so let's put it in its context.

Ever since Adam and Eve in the Garden of Eden, God has been pursuing an intimate personal relationship with mankind. I refer to it as a "conversational relationship." It is a person-to-person relationship of communication, love and obedience. Unfortunately, mankind consistently turned away from God, yet God continued to try to draw His people back to such a relationship. The encounter we are about to examine represents His last corporate try with the people of Israel.

The story goes like this:

And the LORD said to Moses, "Go to the people and consecrate them today and tomorrow. Have them wash their clothes and be ready by the third day, because on that day the LORD will come down on Mount Sinai <u>in the sight of all the people.</u>" Exodus 19:10-11 [Note the phrase; "in the sight of all the people"]

God is saying, "Get the people prepared. In three days, I am going to make My presence known in the sight of all the people. Have the people get prepared. I am going to be with them, ALL of them! I am going to reveal Myself." Previously, Moses asked God to show him His glory? Now is the time it is going to happen for everyone!

One of the instructions that God gave Moses to prepare the people for His coming is a strange one. For years I didn't understand it.

"After Moses had gone down the mountain to the people, he consecrated them, and they washed their clothes. Then he said to the people, "Prepare yourselves for the third day. <u>Abstain from sexual relations</u>." Exodus 19:14-15

He is talking to married couples here, yet He is telling them to abstain from sexual relations. Why? God is the author of sex. This is sex within marriage, so why would He tell them to abstain? I think the answer is that God is coming to reveal Himself to His people - to be intimate with them - and He doesn't want any competing intimacy to interfere with it. Any other intimacy would be a distraction from the intimacy He is offering. His heart is to come and love His people directly – heart to heart. What Moses longed for is now for everyone! God is planning a world changing, history changing, and paradigm changing encounter! It is hard to overstate the importance of what God is offering the people!

Let's set the stage. The third day has come:

On the morning of the third day there was thunder and lightning, with a thick cloud over the mountain, and a very loud trumpet blast. Exodus 19:16

God hasn't even shown up yet and there is smoke and lightning. God's PR people do a pretty good job of portraying His glory. He hasn't even arrived yet and Mount Sinai is in convulsions! The fact is you can't have an encounter in which you actually see the Creator of the universe without it being an awe-inspiring experience. God has not even arrived, and they are terrified. What would the fullness of His glory be like?

Here is something intriguing; the people are full of fear, but Moses is not. Why is Moses unafraid? I think it is because Moses has come to know God as "Friend." His relationship started with a burning bush, which is a pretty awe-inspiring experience, but it quickly progressed into a relationship of intimate friendship. As Moses grew in his experience with God, he experienced a growing desire to see Him as He truly was - in all His glory. Moses had already received this experience and so he had no fear when God began to reveal Himself in a similar way at Sinai.

What is the difference between Moses' reaction to the presence of God and the people? I suppose the difference would be somewhat like the difference between being invited into the Oval Office to meet with the President of the United States verses being his 6-year-old son who wanders in with an "owie." Moses' relationship with God makes the glory no less glorious, but approachable through a depth of knowing that only intimacy can bring.

The story continues:

"Then Moses led the people out of the camp to meet with God, and they stood at the foot of the mountain. Mount Sinai was covered with smoke, because the LORD

descended on it in fire. The smoke billowed up from it like smoke from a furnace, the whole mountain trembled violently, and the sound of the trumpet grew louder and louder. Then Moses spoke, and the voice of God answered him." Exodus 19:17-19

Now at this point in the narrative Moses, inserts the 10 commandments. He puts them in as if that is the next thing that happens chronologically - the people all come out, they are standing around, there is fire and smoke and then suddenly, God gives Moses the 10 commandments.

That is not what happened chronologically. Good biblical scholarship tells us otherwise. If I take my NIV Study Bible and turn to the passage, the footnote at the bottom of the page says that what Moses did at this point in his narrative was to take the 10 commandments and insert them into the story line here, so that they would stand out from the many pages of commentary which follow the 10 commandments.

Moses wanted the 10 commandments to stand out in the story line like a diamond in a setting of gold. He wanted the Ten Commandments to be obviously pre-eminent to the commentary that elaborates upon them. To accomplish this, he took the 10 commandments and inserted them into the story at this point, but this is not chronologically correct. Good evangelical scholarship says the chronology goes like this: Let's read from Exodus 19:18 and skip over to Exodus 20:18-19. Note the seamless flow of events.

"Mount Sinai was covered with smoke, because the LORD descended on it in fire. The smoke billowed up from it like smoke from a furnace, the whole mountain trembled violently... [Exodus 20:18-19] When the people saw the thunder and lightning and heard the trumpet and saw the mountain in smoke, they trembled with fear. They stayed

at a distance and said to Moses, 'Speak to us yourself and we will listen. But do not have God speak to us or we will die.'"

It is easy to see, if you lift out the Ten Commandments, how the story proceeds chronologically.

Now we can see that something very important is happening here. The people are rejecting God! He is coming to reveal Himself and have intimacy with His people. He is just about there. The herald of His arrival, the power of His presence, is beginning to manifest itself and the people fall into fear. They say to Moses, "Don't let Him talk to us, you talk to us. We don't want Him, He is terrifying - you talk to us!" The people rejected a personal relationship with God!

The people remained at a distance, while Moses approached the thick darkness where God was. It is at this point that The Law was given. The Law was given **after** the people had rejected intimacy with the Father. I believe the Law was given as a **consequence** of the people rejecting relationship with God. This is a profound thing! The consequence of rejecting intimacy with the Father is The Law.

It is important to note that the people did not reject God entirely. They rejected a relationship of intimacy with Him, but they still wanted His blessing, protection, and guidance. They just didn't want Him personally. They chose an intermediary – Moses.

What happens when you choose to keep the holiness of God, but reject a personal relationship with God? You get the burden of His holiness, His standards, and trying to measure up to who He is, but you don't get His presence and intimacy. You get His holiness without His empowering presence. You get the requirements of His holiness without the ability to fulfill them.

Let's pause for a moment and let the seriousness of this dawn on us.

The consequence of rejecting intimacy and relationship with God is The Law. It is a life under law. It is religion.

The only thing you are left with when you reject relationship with Him, but want the rest of Him, are the requirements of His holiness – life under The Law.

This puts the people of Israel in the same position as all the rest of the world's religions – under the requirements of a perfect God without the ability to measure up to those requirements.

Moses sees the problem and tries to talk the people out of their decision.

Moses said to the people, **"Do not be afraid. God has come to test you, so that the fear of God will be with you to keep you from sinning."** Exodus 20:20

When I used to read this verse, it was in the understanding of someone who was living under law. I would read it and say, "I know what Moses is saying; God has come to test them and show them what terrible sinners they are so that the fear of God will be in them. They will be so afraid of Him and His judgment that they won't sin. Fear will keep them from sinning - the fear of punishment." And this is how many of us see God and His law; someone to be afraid of, and impossibly hard rules to keep. But is this really what Moses was trying to say?

If you look up the Hebrew words used in this verse you will find that the word "test" does not mean a pass/fail test. It means to "assay" something, like a metal, in order to reveal what is in it. The idea is to make plain the inner qualities of something. When God "tests" you He is coming to reveal something to you about yourself. He is coming to reveal your nature to you so that the fear of God will be in you. So far so good, but what about the meaning of the word "fear."

As good legalists we usually reason that the fear of God must be the fear of His punishment. Upon studying the word "fear" used here, I found that it really has nothing to do with the fear of punishment. "Fear" here refers to that reaction of awe and reverence that I spoke of earlier.

It could be better translated as saying, "The awesome beauty and revealed glory and wonder of God will be with you and that experience, and that knowledge of Him, will discourage sin in you." It is the awesome beauty of God and the revelation of that awesome beauty that keeps us from sinning. Literally "wonder-full."

God is coming to reveal Himself to His people. If they could see Him for a moment, what would result? If they could catch a glimpse of His beauty and glory, even for a moment, the people would be so affected by it that they would not want to sin. If you ever see Him as He is, that revelation of His beauty will so touch you that the last thing in the world you will want to do is leave that moment to run out and sin.

Despite the wonder of this truth, the people said "no" to that and the next thing that happened was God gave them The Law. For the rest of the Old Testament, they lived under The Law rather than in intimacy with Him.

The people rejected God and accepted a substitute. They accepted a representation of Him rather than Him. They kept His truth without His intimacy. They kept His holiness without His Fatherhood. They have His ethics without His indwelling. They have a representative, they have a leader, they have prophets, but they don't have Him. Worse, they have the requirements of His holiness without the indwelling power of

His Spirit that comes with intimacy with Him. They have a religion without a relationship.

So, what does this have to do with positional leadership? The answer comes when we consider the difference between external and internal control of human behavior.

Internal verses external control

Likely you have heard, seen or read, an interview with some highly successful [and wealthy] founder of a well-known business who said something like this, "I never set out to make a lot of money, I just wanted to see my dream become a reality." I have heard many of these and this theme continues to come up – it's not about the money, it's about the dream, and the money isn't the dream. What we are hearing is the difference between an internal versus an external motivation. External controls [or motivations] are what happen **to** us and internal controls [or motivations] are what happen **within** us.

External controls [or motivations] are what happen to us and internal controls [or motivations] are what happen within us.

When a behavior is externally motivated it only occurs while the external force is present. Remove the external force and behavior returns to that which is internally motivated. Everyone who has had children understands how this works. Mom tells Tommy not to take a cookie from the jar. Tommy wants the cookie with all his three-year-old heart, but as long as mommy is in the kitchen, the cookie is safe. As soon as mommy leaves the room Tommy's internal motivation takes over…

External motivation works through only two things, fear and/or reward. The fear can be as to some form of punishment [a fine or jail] or it can be as to the loss of something of deep

67

inner value [damage to one's reputation]. Reward is always a promise to further an inner value. This could be money, not for its own sake, but to fulfill that lifelong desire to have a sailboat [just for the pleasure of being on the water]. It could be the reward of fame which will fulfill the inner value of significance or self-worth. No matter whether it is fear or reward, the goal of external control is altered behavior. At the risk of redundancy, it is important to note that when the external control is absent, the behavior will revert to the deeper and more genuine internal motivation. Put another way, when external control is removed, we find out what is in the heart. We discover our true desires and intentions, and our behavior becomes truest to ourselves, for better or for worse.

Perhaps now we can see the tragedy of Israel's rejection of God at Mt. Sinai. God was offering an intimate relationship of love to every person in Israel. Had they accepted His overture of love; they would have received the ultimate internal motivator - perfect, limitless, divine love. Instead, they received the ultimate external motivator - the law. A quick reading of Leviticus will bring home to our minds the terrible burden of external motivation. Life under the law is a life lived in the fear of failure and the punishment that will follow in the event of failure [which failure is inevitable].

> **When external control is removed, we find out what is in the heart. We discover our true desires and intentions, and our behavior becomes truest to ourselves, for better or worse.**

Positional leadership and law

Now to apply all this to the issue of positional leadership: Positional leadership is impossible without law. Without the threat of punishment or the promise of reward, positional leadership alone has no motivating power. Positional leadership bends the wills of those it leads, by force or manipulation. It has no power to create or alter the internal motivation of those being led. This explains why, after the death of a godly positional leader, the people could so quickly revert to ungodly behavior. Their hearts were never changed. Law does not alter the heart; it merely dominates the will.

The Apostle Paul's understanding of life under law is consistent with the conclusion that law cannot impart holiness or create righteousness:

Without the threat of punishment or the promise of reward, positional leadership alone has no motivating power.

"...the people of Israel, who pursued the law as the way of righteousness, have not attained their goal." Romans 9:31

"... if righteousness could be gained through the law, Christ died for nothing!" Galatians 2:21

"...if a law had been given that could impart life, then righteousness would certainly have come by the law." Galatians 3:21

The only tool available for pure positional leadership to achieve its goals is law, backed by the fear of punishment or the promise of reward. It should be obvious that positional leadership is the least godly, and hence the least effective form of leadership. The history of Israel is the history of the failure of positional leadership.

The only tool available for pure positional leadership to achieve its goals is law, backed by the fear of punishment or the promise of reward.

Despite this fact, many churches today cling to positional leadership and use the Old

Testament model of positional leadership to justify its use in the present-day church. This mistake is only possible if one has an incomplete understanding of the New Covenant.

The New Covenant is the promise of a new way of relating to God, but it also has implications for how we lead God's people. At the heart of the New Covenant is this description of it:

"This is the covenant I will make with the people of Israel after that time," declares the LORD. "I will put my law in their minds and write it on their hearts. I will be their God, and they will be my people. No longer will they teach their neighbor, or say to one another, 'Know the LORD,' because they will all know me, from the least of them to the greatest," declares the LORD. "For I will forgive their wickedness and will remember their sins no more." Jeremiah 31:33-34

Often, we put the emphasis of this verse on the last sentence, focusing on the forgiveness of sin. This is, of course, one of the principle effects of the New Covenant. We rightly call it grace, and we celebrate it. Yet, it is not the whole story of the New Covenant.

The New Covenant delivers a new way to live because it internalizes our motivation for obedience. God's law is now "in our minds and written on our hearts." And the "law" written on our minds and hearts is not some sort of memorized summary of the 10 commandments and the book of Leviticus.

> The New Covenant delivers a new way to live because it internalizes our motivation for obedience. God's law is now "in our minds and written on our hearts."

The "law" of God written in our minds and hearts is the indwelling Holy Spirit. He is within us guiding us into godly thoughts and actions. It is not an external

70

relationship with a code of behavior. It is an internal relationship with a love so powerful it displaces our selfish nature, often without our conscious awareness.

It is an inner transformation of holiness which we cannot take credit for, hence we call it "grace." It is His presence, through His Holy Spirit, that is working at the deepest part of ourselves, quietly, without threat or manipulation, to conform our deepest desires to His desires for us. And His desires for us are always consistent with our greatest capacity for joy! Isn't He wonderful!

Dallas Willard describes this transformation Jesus came to bring as a "revolution."

"The revolution of Jesus is in the first place and continuously a revolution of the human heart or spirit. It did not and does not proceed by means of the formation of social institutions and laws, the outer forms of our existence, intending that these would then impose a good order of life upon people who come under their power. Rather, his is a revolution of character, which proceeds by changing people from the inside through ongoing personal relationship to God in Christ and to one another."[12]

He goes on to emphasize the internal aspect of Christian transformation and learning by saying:

"...I must reemphasize, because it is so important – the primary "learning" here is not about how to act, just as the primary wrongness or problem in human life is not what we do. Often what human beings do is so horrible that we can be excused, perhaps, for thinking that all that matters is stopping it. But this is an evasion of the real horror: the heart from which the terrible actions come. In both cases, it is who we are in our thoughts, feelings, disposition and choices – in the inner life – that counts. Profound transformation there is the only thing that can

definitively   conquer   outward   evil."[13]

This kind of transformation is completely inconsistent with positional leadership. This transformation comes about through divine influence. Here is how I have described it elsewhere:

The way God leads us is a wonderful example of His reluctance to use His positional authority over us. There is little doubt in any Christian's mind that God has the right [as creator of the universe] to issue commands which should be obeyed without question or delay. He has the ultimate positional authority as King, and this is the way we should expect Him to lead us – by command.

As I was thinking about this, I began to examine all the ways God has led me from the time of my conversion. I was trying to remember any time God led me by command. I could not think of even one.

During the last year I have had the opportunity to question several hundred Christians in several different churches. Through a questionnaire, I asked them to go through their memories to find instances of God leading through a command, e.g. "Do this because I am God and I command you to!" Only 21% answered that God had ever led them by command. Of these, the instances of God leading by command was less than 5% [in other words 95% of the time God led them through influence rather than by command].

As we examine how God has consistently led us, we find that it has been largely through influence rather than command.

As we examine how God has consistently led us, we find that it has been largely through influence rather than command. What do I mean by influence? Here is a scripture to help us answer this question:

"For it is God who is at work in you, enabling you both to will and to work for His good pleasure." Phil. 2:13

This verse yields significant insight when we consider the meaning of the words "to will" used to describe the part of our being that God "enables" to do His good pleasure. The word "will" used here refers to the deepest part of our personality where our deepest desires are found. This verse is telling us that God's Spirit, living at the deepest level of our desires, influences our desires gently and quietly until we find ourselves desiring what He desires for us. It is often so subtle and gentle that we usually believe the desire was our idea.

Here is a humorous personal example:

"Years ago, Shell and I took a sabbatical in San Diego for 5 months of the Canadian winter - clearly God's will! It was a wonderful time, but I missed my home church, our house, etc. The next year we did it again. About halfway through our second winter in San Diego, Shell told me she wanted to move to San Diego permanently.

I was dead set against a move. I was genuinely upset by the idea. I asked her not to speak to me about it again. I further told her to talk to God about it and if He wanted us here, He would change my heart without her involvement! Without telling me, she set out to do just that. I was happy with my spiritual leadership of the marriage and happily put the matter out of my mind – job done!

I remember the moment clearly. About two weeks later we were driving south on the 15 freeway and out of my mouth came the strangest words. I said, "I really want to move here!" My desire was perfectly sincere and genuine. I had expressed my deepest desire and it came as a surprise to me. I had not reasoned out the pros and cons like I usually would. I just knew I wanted to move. The next year we did, and we have been happy with our new home ever since."[14] [Paraphrased from Reluctantly Supernatural p. 225-228]

One of the things I appreciate most about our Father is that He would rather lead us through His quiet influence within us than through His commands. Perhaps this is because **commands are very effective in the short run, but do not lead to real transformation of the heart.**

We have all experienced something like this; your boss [parent, teacher, coach] enters the room and gives you a command. You obey because he is standing watching you, but as soon as he leaves the room, you revert to doing what you really wanted to do.

Simple obedience to commands does not transform the heart. God is far more interested in transforming you at the level of your deepest desires than in simply getting you to do the right thing. He does not simply want your reluctant obedience; He wants you to become a person who wants the things that are truly best for you and the rest of His children. Isn't He wonderful!

> God is far more interested in transforming you at the level of your deepest desires than in simply getting you to do the right thing.

Life in the Holy Spirit

Another way of explaining the New Covenant is by understanding the role of the Holy Spirit in the New Covenant life of a Christian. Jesus promised us the indwelling Holy Spirit who would **"guide you into all the truth"**. [John 16:13] Jesus is promising a guidance beyond that of the law. Paul explains it this way.

"You, however, are controlled not by the sinful nature but by the Spirit..." [Rom. 8:9]

Jesus uses the word "guide" and Paul uses the word "control" but taken together they amount to influence. There is no connotation of the use of force or threat to guide or lead.

We must not forget that the promised Holy Spirit is living within each of us. He guides and leads from **within** us. This is the opposite of any kind of external control. Given the fact of the indwelling Holy Spirit within us, leadership through positional authority [external control] is no longer valid as the principle form of leadership in the New Testament church age in which we live. It is time to explore and define leadership through influence, but first...

Some Questions to Consider:

1. How would you define the difference between external and internal control of behavior?

2. In your experience, how often has God used external control to control your decisions/behavior?

3. In your experience, how often does external control determine your decisions/behavior?

4. Why do you think God prefers to use His influence to affect your decisions rather than force?

5. How has God used internal motivation to guide you?

6. "Law does not alter the heart; it merely dominates the will." Agree or disagree? Why?

7. How do you want to lead others?

8. Why do you think positional leadership remains the "go to" leadership method?

SECTION TWO -

THE NEW DEAL

Chapter 6: New Testament Models of Influential Leadership

"I want you to want me.
I need you to need me.
I'd love you to love me.

Rick Nielsen, Cheap Trick, 1977

This is technically a love song, but it is not about a love that exists. It is about a love that is longed for. The writer is longing for a girl he has fallen in love with, but she has not returned his love. These are simple lyrics, but profound in their implication.

The sad truth is that we can always long for love, but we cannot always make it happen. The best a lover can do is to prove his love to the one he loves and hope that it is returned. He cannot use force because that would be inconsistent with love. He cannot use deceit for the same reason. Nor can he use money to buy her love. All he can do is woo her. All he has at his disposal is influence.

The Merriam-Webster dictionary defines influence as 1. "the act or power of producing an effect without apparent force or direct authority." & 2. "the power or capacity of causing an effect in indirect or intangible ways."

Why did I start this chapter with a love song? Because our King is the perfect lover. He doesn't just love us, He IS love. We were created by love, to love, for love. Love requires freedom and so He set us free from His positional authority so that we could love Him freely. Of course, we would be wise to love Him because of His positional authority as King, but we don't have to. Because He IS love, His means for bringing us into a relationship of love with Him are never inconsistent with love.

This means that like the lover we have just described, God will not use force or His positional authority to compel us to return His love. This leaves Him with influence. **His influence is the power of His perfect love.**

I suppose we could suggest that after we have fallen in love with Him and the love relationship has been established, He could begin to lead us through His positional authority - by command. Yet, this won't work because to habitually lead another through command or force is to cease to love.

Of course, there are times when out of love for a child, a parent will violate the child's will to save her from serious harm, but in a loving relationship this is the exception rather than the rule. If this is true, then we should expect to see God leading His children [under the New Covenant] through influence [through love] rather than through positional authority. We should expect to see Jesus leading this way, and we should expect to see the human leaders of the New Testament church leading this way as well. So, let's see if our expectations are justified. Let's start with Jesus.

Jesus' model of leadership

Who is Jesus? When we think of Jesus the words that most often come to mind are: King of Kings, Lord of Lords, Savior, and Master. All these are accurate and true descriptions of Him, but they do not accurately describe Him in His ministry as a human among humans. These terms are descriptions of His divinity but what was His principle identity as a human – while He lived as the Godman on earth? Through what identity or attitude did He see himself? Another way to ask the question is to ask, "What is the difference in His identity between His first and second coming?"

The writer of the Book of Philippians answers this question for us:

"In your relationships with one another, have the same mindset as Christ Jesus: Who, being in very nature God, did not consider equality with God something to be used to his own advantage; rather, he made himself nothing by taking the very nature of a servant, being made in human likeness." [Phil. 2:5-7]

"He made himself nothing, taking the very nature of a servant" – strong words indeed! Jesus' chosen identity, and principle role in His dealings with His Father God and His fellow humans, was as a servant. To understand His leadership model, we need to keep His primary identity continually in mind. He is the greatest leader who ever lived. At the same time, He is the greatest servant who ever lived. Combining these two roles together we arrive at Jesus' model of leadership – servant leadership.

We must not forget that it was Jesus who chose the role of servant leader. "He made himself nothing" was His choice. It was not something His Father commanded Him to do. In choosing to lead humanity to God, Jesus chose to do it through the role of a servant. Counterintuitive, isn't it?

Counterintuitive possibly, but the choice is entirely consistent with God's choice to lead us through influence rather than positional authority. Jesus has the positional authority to lead through a command structure, but most of the time He leads by example and through influence.

Jesus delegates His leadership model to His leaders in training

When Jesus chose His 12 disciples, He chose 12 Jewish men. As Jews, their concept of leadership was shaped by the Old Testament and the leadership structure found in the synagogue. As a result, their understanding of "godly" leadership was primarily positional. Their leaders lorded it over them. Not only was it their religious understanding of leadership, but their secular as well. They lived under the Roman occupation where they were an oppressed nation. In order to assure that His leaders in training understood His new model of leadership, Jesus had to be very direct. This is what we see Jesus doing after the mother of Zebedee's sons comes to Jesus asking that He sit her two sons on His left and right, when He takes His throne.

"When the ten heard about this, they were indignant with the two brothers. Jesus called them together and said, "You know that the rulers of the Gentiles lord it over them, and their high officials exercise authority over them. Not so with you. Instead, whoever wants to become great among you must be your servant, and whoever wants to be first must be your slave— just as the Son of Man did not come to be served, but to serve, and to give his life as a ransom for many." Matthew 20:24-28

Jesus goes so far as to use the term "slave" to emphasize the kind of servant leadership he is delegating them to.

Jesus calls us to the same kind of servant leadership

It would be convenient and tempting for us to suggest that although Jesus called His first disciples to servant leadership, there is no evidence that He intends the same for us today. Could servant leadership still be His choice for us 2000 years later?

The answer to this question is found in what we call the "great commission" in Matthew Chapter 28:18-20. The usual lesson extracted from this passage focuses on evangelism – "go and make disciples of all nations." What we often miss is that Jesus is not commissioning us to make converts but rather disciples. Discipleship is the goal; evangelism is merely the first step.

Fortunately for us, Jesus defines discipleship in this passage when He says, "...**make disciples of all nations, baptizing them in the name of the Father and of the Son and of the Holy Spirit, and <u>teaching them to obey everything I have commanded you</u>**." Matthew 28:19-20

We have already seen that Jesus taught His disciples to lead as servants not as overlords. This passage is more than enough proof text to establish Jesus' model of leadership for us today. We stand in a line of delegated spiritual authority, teaching, example, and command that started 2000 years ago in Matthew 28 and which will endure until Jesus' second coming. Servant leadership is a command, not just to His first disciples, but also to every disciple after them. But wait... there's more...

As will be discussed later, leading by example is an integral part of servant leadership. It is a way that influence is increased in a leader. For this reason, Jesus was not content with merely verbally instructing His disciples in the model of servant leadership, He lived it by way of example. This is best exemplified when Jesus washed the disciples' feet. There is so much of value to our understanding of leadership through influence that it is worth examining the story in detail:

"**It was just before the Passover Festival. Jesus knew that the hour had come for him to leave this world and go to the Father. Having loved his own who were in the world, he now showed them the full extent of His love. The evening meal was in progress, and the devil had already prompted Judas, the son of Simon Iscariot, to betray Jesus. Jesus knew that the Father had put all things under his power, and that he had come from God and was returning to God; so, he got up from the meal, took off his outer clothing, and wrapped a towel around his waist. After that, he poured water into a basin and began to wash his disciples' feet, drying them with the towel that was wrapped around him... When he had finished washing** their feet, he put on his clothes and returned to his place. "Do you understand what I have done for you?" he asked them. "You call me 'Teacher' and 'Lord,' and rightly so, for I have set you an example that you should do as I have done for you. Very truly I tell you, no servant is greater than his master, nor is a messenger greater than the one who sent him. Now that you know these things, you will be blessed if you do them." John 13:1-17

There is much more going on in this story than simply Jesus providing a lesson in servant leadership by way of example. Before we read of Jesus' example of servant leadership, we should first discover His motivation and empowerment for taking the role of a servant leader.

Jesus' motivation

The story begins with Jesus' motivation for humbling himself in order to serve His followers. He had loved them up until this moment, but now He is going to "show them the full extent of His love." The motivation for being a servant leader must always be love. Any other motivation results in actions which are manipulative. I have heard poor leaders excuse manipulative leadership as necessary for the "good of the church." Somehow the "church" becomes an institution rather than a community of individuals in need of love.

All of Jesus' teaching was so that our "joy might increase", even when He was bringing correction or discipline. Even while angry and driving the money changers from the temple, His motivation was His love for people. His truth was always delivered in a container of love. A servant without love is a slave to some motive other than love. Such a leader is outside of the heart of Jesus.

Jesus' empowerment for being a servant leader

Seeing oneself as the servant of all requires a supremely secure self-image. The foregoing passage shows us the source of Jesus' empowerment necessary to take

Seeing oneself as the servant of all requires a supremely secure self-image.

the identity of a servant. One little two letter word reveals the source of Jesus' empowerment... "so." "Jesus knew that the Father had put all things under His power, and that He had come from God and was returning to God; **so**... He began to wash His disciples' feet..."

Jesus deepest identity is not as a servant but as a son. Jesus is rooted in the love of the Father. Only by drawing from the Father's love and approval can Jesus humble himself before broken and sinful men. The same is true for all leaders.

A leader who is not secure in the Father's love will suffer from the fear of man. His reaction to this fear will either be to take shelter in his positional authority and become a manipulator, or to become an ineffectual people pleaser.

For all those gifted as leaders and aspiring to leadership, there is nothing more important than your hidden relationship with your Father God. This is where true security comes from. If that relationship is healthy, servant leadership will come naturally.

Jesus' Humility

Inherent in the foregoing discussion of Jesus' identity as a servant leader is His humility. The Philippian passage we quoted earlier tells us that in coming to live as a man on earth Jesus "humbled himself." Jesus' entire life was lived in humility - by His own choice. It is tempting to forget just how radical a choice this must have been. John tells us that through Jesus **"all**

things were made; without Him nothing was made that has been made." John 1:3

Here is the creator choosing to submit Himself to His creation. He not only becomes a part of it, He submits to the worst of it. Even before an ungodly secular authority, which is about to sentence Him to death, He submits to it, resulting in His complete humiliation and death.

Jesus lived humility in every action and every word He spoke. His goal was always to bring honor to His Father and the Holy Spirit. Whenever He was glorified by men, He turned the attention toward His Father or the Holy Spirit. He became completely submitted to His Father's will and He made Himself completely dependent upon the power of the Holy Spirit.

As a young Christian I used to question the humility of God. How can the creator of the universe be humble? The answer of course is that our God is not one, but three. Our God is a relationship of love. Each one of the three is in love with the other two. Each one lives to give glory to the other two. Jesus is always diverting attention toward the Father and Holy Spirit. The Father is always saying "look at my Son, listen to Him." Jesus tells His disciples that it is good that He is leaving them because when He goes, they will receive the Holy Spirit. And the Holy Spirit lives to reveal Jesus. The Trinity is love, in love, with love.

The Apostle Paul tells us in the Philippians passage already quoted that we should have the same attitude of humility that Jesus had – a voluntary choice to humble ourselves. This is so for all Christians, but particularly

The choice to be a servant leader is the most effective prophylactic we have against pride. In our minds the word "servant" must always come before the word "leader."

difficult for leaders. Because of the position of authority given to leaders, pride is a constant companion and a constant temptation.

The choice to be a servant leader is a daily one and we require a daily reminder of its importance. The choice to be a servant leader is the most effective prophylactic we have against pride. In our minds the word "servant" must always come before the word "leader."

"If you become a leader before you become a servant, you will use your talent to move people to fulfill your agenda regardless of their well-being. You will see and treat people as cogs in your wheel to move and use as you deem necessary. If you become a servant before you become a leader, you will see your talent as a gift to be used for the good of others. You will see yourself as a servant to a higher calling; a more noble mission; a purpose greater than yourself. The power of a servant leader does not come from their position but from their sacrifice."[15] Pastor Erwin R. McManus, Mosaic Church, Los Angeles,

The sad fact is that positional leadership empowers our pride.

Positional leadership is most often driven by the leader's "vision." The leader believes the vision came from God, and usually it did. The leader's temptation at this point is to see the people as the resources, given him by God, to fulfill the vision. More times than I can count I have heard pastors refer to the members of their congregation as "the people God has given me." With this belief the positional leader now has a perfect justification for treating the people as nothing more than resources.

I have never heard a pastor refer to the congregation he leads as the people to whom God has given him.

86

I have never heard a pastor refer to the congregation he leads as the people to whom God has given him.

Pride takes advantage of this faulty reasoning by telling the leader, "You are doing God's work! You are serving the people by giving them an opportunity to be a part of a great vision from God. You are the general and they are your foot soldiers. You are special! Your needs come first. Without you and your vision, the people parish."

What every positional leader needs to remember is that God's "vision" defines not merely the goal, but also the means to follow to achieve the goal. In every vision from God, the people are the vision. Any vision that results in "using" people is not a godly vision.

The unique temptation for every visionary leader is using people as resources rather than serving them as individuals. This temptation comes to all of us as members of the first world. Francis Frangipane explains it this way,

"Part of our problem is the affluent world in which we live. We are served by hundreds of non-human "slaves," remarkable mechanical devices created just to serve us. Our slaves do laundry, clean dishes, figure out bookkeeping and entertain us. They carry us across town and country – and for all they do, we are offended if their service does not meet or exceed our expectations. Jesus said the greatest among us would be servant of all. [see Matthew 23:11; Mark 10:43-44] We in our modern world have things reversed – we are the ones who are supposed to be the slaves. It is only our pride that thinks otherwise."[16]

Before we go on to examine the characteristics of leadership through influence, we need to examine the Apostle Paul's attitude toward godly leadership. Does Paul's teaching and his example agree with Jesus' view of servant leadership?

We cannot neglect Paul's example because, apart from Jesus, Paul is the premier leader of the New Testament church. Apart from his theology of grace and his ministry to the Gentiles we Gentiles would be excluded from God's plan of salvation. I would not have written this book, and you would not be reading it. On to Paul! But first...

Some Questions to Consider:

1. I have said that "God's influence is the power of His perfect love." Have you experienced this influence over your motivations? When was the last time you experienced His love?

2. Why is love inconsistent with control most of the time?

2. When is control an act of love?

3. Where did Jesus [the man] obtain the strength to become the servant of all?

4. Can you explain how Jesus calls us, who are living today, to servant leadership?

5. Jesus' identity as a servant was based upon His identity as His Father's well-loved child. Is this same identity operating in your life?

6. What will it take for you to assume the identity of a servant to those God has given you to?

7. In your experience, how often is having a "vision" an excuse for a leader "using" people?

Chapter 7: The Apostle Paul's Leadership Model

Jesus chose to come to earth as a servant. He taught His disciples to choose to see themselves likewise. Jesus established the foundation of His church and Paul built on it. This raises two questions; did Paul build the Gentile church [of which we are a part] in conformity to Jesus' model of servant leadership? And how did Paul see himself as a leader?

How a person describes himself as a leader is usually a good indication of his philosophy of leadership. Paul wrote 13 books of the New Testament. In 8 of them he introduced himself as an "apostle of Christ Jesus" or an "apostle of Jesus Christ." Being an apostle of Jesus Christ is Paul's primary identity as a leader.

An "apostle" is defined as "a delegate, messenger, one sent forth with orders." As used by Paul in the early church, it is not an honorific title, but rather a description of his function. He is literally, "the one Jesus sent with a message." By using this term, he is saying no more than that he is a messenger from Jesus.

In two books he describes himself as a servant of Christ Jesus or a servant of God. The word Paul is using here for "servant" is a very strong word. It translates as: "a delegate, messenger, one sent forth with orders", "a slave, bondman, man of servile condition", "one devoted to another to the disregard of one's own interest" & "a slave." There is no connotation of positional authority suggested or implied. There is a real lack of ego in Paul's writing, despite facts that would make Paul susceptible to it.

More than any other writer of the New Testament Paul has the right to boast. As a theologian he is in a class by himself. Through his theology, Christianity is defined by grace and thus separates itself from all other world religions. His education and religious background are unequaled. In his own words.

"...If someone else thinks they have reasons to put confidence in the flesh, I have more: circumcised on the eighth day of the people of Israel, of the tribe of Benjamin, a Hebrew of Hebrews; in regard to the law, a Pharisee; as for zeal, persecuting the church; as for righteousness based on the law, faultless. But whatever were gains to me I now consider loss for the sake of Christ. What is more, I consider everything a loss because of the surpassing worth of knowing Christ Jesus my Lord, for whose sake I have lost all things. I consider them garbage, that I may gain Christ and be found in him, not having a righteousness of my own that comes from the law, but that which is through faith in Christ—the righteousness that comes from God on the basis of faith." Phil. 3:4-9

All his many qualifications he considers garbage in comparison to knowing Jesus. This is clear evidence of a lack of self-focus, rare in our Christian world of leaders. There is no salesmanship in Paul.

Later in the book we will discuss the role that self-awareness plays in the life of an influential leader, and how it is related to humility, but for now we will examine three examples of Paul's self-awareness and the humility it brings.

"For I am the least of the apostles and do not even deserve to be called an apostle, because I persecuted the church of God." 1 Cor. 15:9

"Although I am less than the least of all the Lord's people, this grace was given me: to preach to the Gentiles the boundless riches of Christ," Eph. 3:8

"Even if I should choose to boast, I would not be a fool, because I would be speaking the truth. But I refrain, so no one will think more of me than is warranted by what I do or say, or because of these surpassingly great revelations. Therefore, in order to keep me from becoming conceited, I was given a thorn in my flesh, a messenger of Satan, to torment me. Three times I pleaded with the Lord to take it away from me. But he said to me, "My grace is sufficient for you, for my power is made perfect in weakness." Therefore, I will boast all the more gladly about my weaknesses, so that Christ's power may rest on me. That is why, for Christ's sake, I delight in weaknesses, in insults, in hardships, in persecutions, in difficulties. For when I am weak, then I am strong." 2 Cor. 12:6-10

As the third passage indicates, Paul has every reason to boast in both his giftedness and his amazing spiritual experiences. As well, he also recognizes that even if he chose to boast it would amount to nothing more than telling the truth. Despite this, Paul sees pride waiting at his door and he sees God's remedy – "a thorn in my flesh, a messenger of Satan, to torment me."

Paul is so aware of the destructive nature of pride, and his susceptibility to it, that he chooses to welcome the humility that comes by enduring the torment. Here is a leader who truly knows his weaknesses as well as his strengths. Paul's solution is to replace boasting in his strengths with boasting in his weaknesses because God's

Paul is so aware of the destructive nature of pride, and his susceptibility to it, that he chooses to welcome the humility that comes by enduring the torment.

strength is glorified in overcoming Paul's weaknesses.

Paul is as aware of his weaknesses as he is of his strengths. He has no difficulty being honest with himself AND others about them. Pride demands that we ignore our weaknesses and hide them whenever possible. This results in leaders who do not consider their weaknesses when making momentous decisions. Real humility is being as aware of one's weaknesses as one's strengths. More on this later when we discuss self-awareness as a characteristic of influential leadership.

Paul avoids positional leadership

At the risk of belaboring the point, Paul has every right to lead the churches he has planted from a position of command. The same can be said of the leaders he has appointed over those churches. In many present-day denominations, they call the founding leader the "Apostle" over that denomination and, in many cases, he is expected to lead by command. But is this positional leadership consistent with the New Testament Church's example? Paul's leadership answers the question in the negative.

I have just concluded a reading of all of Paul's epistles in an attempt to find any example of Paul basing any of his instructions to "his" churches upon his position as Apostle over them. I could not find one. Although he discusses the fact of having planted a given church, he never uses that fact as a reason for its obedience to his instructions.

Paul's principle means of instruction is by way of persuasion. He is a teacher first and foremost, and he uses reason to convince his hearers of the wisdom of his instruction. Beyond persuasion, he uses the fact of his love for those he is leading. He is not hesitant to remind them of how deeply he loves them and how badly he wants the best for them. As well, he is not ashamed to remind them of what he has suffered for their sake.

Beyond appealing to them on the basis of his love for them, he is not ashamed to beg them to follow his instructions.

Here follow some examples of Paul's persuasion, statements of his love, and urging/begging, in order to influence those he leads:

Urging

"Therefore, I urge you, brothers and sisters, in view of God's mercy, to offer your bodies as a living sacrifice, holy and pleasing to God—this is your true and proper worship." Rom. 12:1

"Urge" used here translates as "admonish", "exhort", "entreat", "beseech", "appeal" and "beg." This is not a term of command. Paul uses this term repeatedly throughout his letters:

"I urge you, brothers and sisters, to watch out for those who cause divisions and put obstacles in your way that are contrary to the teaching you have learned..." Rom. 16:17

"I appeal to you, brothers and sisters, in the name of our Lord Jesus Christ, that all of you agree with one another..." 1 Cor. 1:10

The word "appeal" used here is the same Greek word translated as "urge."

"I plead with you, brothers and sisters, become like me, for I became like you." Gal. 4:12 The word used here means to "desire", "long for" or "beg." Again, there is no hint of command.

"I plead with Euodia and I plead with Syntyche to be of the same mind in the Lord." Phil. 4:2 [the same word as "urge"]

"And we <u>urge</u> you, brothers and sisters, warn those who are idle and disruptive, encourage the disheartened, help the weak, be patient with everyone." 1 Thes. 5:14 [the same word as "urge"]

"As I <u>urged</u> you when I went into Macedonia..." 1 Tim. 1:3 [the same word]

"I <u>urge</u>, then, first of all, that petitions, prayers, intercession and thanksgiving be made for all people" 1 Tim. 2:1 [the same word]

Appealing to his love

"For I could wish that I myself were cursed and cut off from Christ for the sake of my people, those of my own race," Rom. 9:3 What a profound expression of love!

"Not that we lord it over your faith, but we work with you for your joy..." 2 Cor. 1:24

"For I wrote you out of great distress and anguish of heart and with many tears, not to grieve you but to let you know the depth of my love for you." 2 Cor. 2:4

Coming as a "father"

"Even if you had ten thousand guardians in Christ, you do not have many fathers, for in Christ Jesus I became your father through the gospel. Therefore, I urge you to imitate me. For this reason, I have sent to you Timothy, my son whom I love, who is faithful in the Lord. He will remind you of my way of life in Christ Jesus, which agrees with what I teach everywhere in every church." 1 Cor. 4:15-17

"As a fair exchange—I speak as to my children—open wide your hearts also." 2 Cor. 6:13

"My dear children, for whom I am again in the pains of childbirth until Christ is formed in you, how I wish I could be with you now and change my tone, because I am perplexed about you!" Gal. 4:19-20

There is one more passage that is particularly revealing of Paul's philosophy of leadership which we should study, but before we conclude with that discussion, here are a few more references that reveal Paul's humility and avoidance of positional leadership:

Paul intentionally chose to come in weakness in order to rely only on the power of the Holy Spirit. 1 Cor. 2:1-5

Paul compares himself to Apollos as an equal rather than as his superior. 1 Cor. 3:1-9

In giving instructions to the single and married Paul is very careful to distinguish between a command of the Lord and his own personal opinion, something many leaders fail to do. 1 Cor. 7:10-12

He does the same in his instructions to virgins where he admits to having no command of the Lord, but simply his opinion. 1 Cor. 7:25

To conclude our examination of Paul's leadership model and philosophy, we will look at Paul's letter to Philemon. The backstory is important to understanding Paul's approach to Philemon. Philemon was a Christian who owned a slave named Onesimus. From what we can deduce from the letter, Onesimus stole from Philemon and ran away. Such action entitled Philemon to kill Onesimus.

While away from his master, Onesimus came under Paul's teaching and became a Christian. In this letter Paul is now arguing for mercy on the basis that Onesimus is now

Philemon's Christian brother. Here are the relevant parts of the letter:

After reminding Philemon of Paul's thanksgiving for Philemon's friendship, and Paul's genuine love for him, Paul goes on to state his case:

"Therefore, although in Christ I could be bold and order you to do what you ought to do, yet **I prefer to appeal to you on the basis of love. It is as none other than Paul — an old man and now also a prisoner of Christ Jesus — that I <u>appeal</u> to you for my son Onesimus, who became my son while I was in chains."** Philemon 1:8-10

This may be the clearest instance of Paul explicitly eschewing his positional authority. He admits that he has it, but he refuses to use it. He comes only in the name of love and as an "old man." [This is probably Paul's attempt at humor, to bring a lighter tone to an otherwise very serious life or death issue.]

Paul is again using the language of appeal [urging] rather than command. Paul continues...

"I am sending him—who is my very heart—back to you. I would have liked to keep him with me so that he could take your place in helping me while I am in chains for the gospel. But I did not want to do anything without your consent, so that any favor you do will be spontaneous and not forced." Philemon 1:12-14

God rarely leads us by command. To do so denies us the benefit of freely giving our obedience.

Paul's last sentence is consistent with the heart of the Father. Paul refused to use his positional authority to accomplish a just and loving result, because to do so would be to deny Philemon his moral freedom. God rarely leads us by command. To do so denies us the benefit of freely giving our obedience. It is the imposition of a stronger will over a weaker tone. It negates the opportunity for moral and spiritual growth in the one being led. To quote the Canadian songwriter, Bruce Cockburn, "You wanted us like you, as choosers not clones."

At the rewards banquet in heaven

I have this scene that plays in my imagination: I see myself before Jesus at the rewards banquet in heaven. Awards for obedience are being given out. I am standing with the people I have led in "my" church. The first guy comes up and Jesus asks him, "what good deeds do you have to present to me for judgement and rewards?" The guy says, "I taught Sunday School for 15 years... with the middle schoolers!" Jesus says, "Wow! What a sacrifice! What prompted you to make that painful sacrifice?" The guy turns and points to me and says, "My pastor made me do it!" Jesus looks at me and I experience His disappointment.

This little story is my attempt at humor, but I am very serious about the point I am trying to make. The good works God is looking for are actions that proceeded from a pure and free heart. Actions which are motivated by selfishness are not godly actions. Neither are actions which arise from guilt, shame or manipulation on the part of a leader. Neither the actor nor the manipulator accumulates points in heaven for these kinds of actions.

It is our human nature to judge an action as good or bad on the basis of its external appearance. God does not make the same mistake. Jesus made this very clear when He said that it is what proceeds from the heart of a person that makes an action good or bad. In God's world motives matter. It is not just a matter of what we do, but why we do it as well.

The application of this truth for leadership is obvious. God is not in the behavior modification business; He is in the heart transformation business. An influential leader will focus on the spiritual state of the person's heart. When the heart changes the behavior will soon follow.

Having said all I have about Paul avoiding his positional authority I might have left you with the idea that Paul abandoned or rejected his positional authority. This is not the case. In 2 Corinthians 13:10 Paul tells the Corinthian church that he has authority over them given to him by God, but he makes it clear that he does not wish to use it harshly.

"This is why I write these things when I am absent, that when I come, I may not have to be harsh in my use of authority – the authority the Lord gave me for building you up, not for tearing you down."

Later in the book we will deal with those circumstances in which positional authority should be used, but for now it is sufficient to remind ourselves that the use of positional authority should be the exception rather than the rule, and influence is the rule.

Now let's look at the characteristics of influential leadership, but first...

Some Questions to Consider:

1. Is it a coincidence that Paul is the author of our theology of grace and also our example of leadership through influence? How are grace and non-positional leadership connected?

2. Give some examples of Paul's self-awareness.

3. What is the role in Paul's life played by his "thorn in the flesh?"

4. What is your "thorn in the flesh?" What role does it play in your life with God?

5. Paul uses persuasion as his "go to" leadership tool. How can you improve your leadership through persuasion?

SECTION THREE -

CHARACTERISTICS OF INFLUENTIAL LEADERSHIP

Chapter 8 – Influence: Competence, Character & Caring

In preparation for this book I created a survey questionnaire which I submitted to hundreds of church-going Christians in multiple denominations. The questionnaire asked the participant to think of a leader, secular or religious, to whom they voluntarily gave influence in their lives. It could be a teacher, coach, boss, parent, friend, etc. Having identified this person I asked them to determine what it was about that person that caused them to give them influence in their lives.

Although the answers were varied, they broke down into three easily identifiable categories: competence, character and caring.

Competence had to do with the skills and success displayed by the influencer. These included financial success, higher education, professional success, spiritual giftedness and the ability to communicate vision.

Character had to do with integrity, truthfulness, leading by example, not asking them to do something the leader was not willing to do himself, self-control, self-awareness, emotional intelligence, and what the Bible calls the "fruits of the Holy Spirit."

Caring had to do with love; being available, approachable, supportive, non-judgmental, listening, & showing a genuine interest in their physical, relational, emotional, financial and spiritual well-being. Generally, all the attitudes and behaviors we would expect from the spiritual calling of "pastor."

What was valuable was determining which of the three was most influential. I have described the survey to many people since its completion and my common questions to each person have been, "what do you think was the most important factor?" And "how would you rank them from least to most influential?" Thus far everyone has ranked them in the same order, and everyone has been correct. From least to most influential they are competence, character and caring. The percentages break down as follows: 8.5%, 38.7% & 52.7% respectively.

The order is what we would expect and is consistent with the maxim "they don't care how much you know until they know how much you care." What is surprising is the very low percentage of respondents who listed competence as the reason for giving a person influence in their lives. **Character exceeds competence by more than 400% and Caring exceeds it by more than 600%!** Character exceeds competence by more than 400% and Caring exceeds it by more than 600%! This is significant because of the amount of attention currently being paid to developing leadership skills which have little to do with character or caring, especially in the church.

Through its various seminaries and Bible schools the Western church graduates potential leaders who are well schooled in Bible study, Hebrew, Greek, and oratory skills. These skills are essential to the successful teaching of the Bible. Unfortunately, much less time is spent in teaching our future teachers in how to acquire a conversational relationship with God. The inner life often suffers when the emphasis is largely upon exegetical and leadership skills.

Recently I was speaking with a friend of mine doing his master's degree at a Christian university. I asked him to review his course load necessary for his degree, to determine the percentage of teaching units devoted to the formation of

Christian character vs. the acquisition of leadership skills. The result was 13% versus 87%.

Interview

I remember a story my mentor told me of a job interview he had with a recent seminary graduate. The seminary in question was the one from which my mentor obtained his PhD. The ministry job applicant spent all the interview time recounting his seminary grades and successes. My mentor ended the interview by telling the applicant that if he was hired, he would try not to hold his seminary degree against him. A joke? Knowing my mentor, probably. But it does beg the question, are we more impressed with skills rather than character? Isn't knowing God more important than knowing about Him?

I am not arguing against good Bible training or academic excellence. I am arguing against holding it in higher esteem than love. Love truly is "the most excellent way."

The remaining chapters of this book will deal with the characteristics of influential leadership and the remainder of this chapter will deal with competence as it supports influence. Because competence is the least important of the sources of influence, we will only deal with it in a cursory manner.

Competence

1. Good Bible Teaching

Good Bible teaching is foundational to the health of every church. We need look no further than the writings of Paul to support this claim. Paul is a master Bible teacher. Logic, great illustrations, personal anecdotes, and analogies common to everyday life make Paul's messages powerful and persuasive. How many times have you asked someone why they like their church and they answered with "the teaching"? For me, more times than I can count.

Leadership by influence is dependent upon being able to persuade people as to what is best for them in their relationship with God. Good teaching is the usual way this persuasion occurs, but it has its limits. A church I visit regularly went through a bad church split a few years ago. Sadly, some good people left the church. About a year ago I was talking to one couple that left and they told me that they had settled at a large mega church – very unlike the smaller church they left. I was curious as to what drew them to this particular church. They told me the Bible teaching was excellent. They said they were very happy there and looked forward to being there for their foreseeable future.

Recently I saw them again, only to find that they had left the large church to attend a smaller church. I asked them why the change. They told me that although the teaching was wonderful, they were never able to make a relational connection with any group of people within the church. What they were missing was the love connection that defines our faith. Teaching alone will not make up for a lack of love.

Despite what I just wrote, teaching is important, so what sort of qualifications are necessary? Opinions vary on this point because people are wired differently. Some are intellectual by nature and are moved by a rational argument. Others are more emotional and want to be stirred by a passionate message. Others love stories and learn best by picturing an unfolding story. No one teacher can be everything to everyone, all the time.

The bottom line is that no teaching should be boring. Bible truths should be presented in the simplest terms common to the average Christian.

Drop the jargon

My goal for a sermon is to use as few technical Christian terms as possible. My target audience is the guy at my gym. He is smart but not religious. If I can explain our faith to him then I know I have communicated it well. The key is to know your congregation. A church attached to a seminary will teach differently than one located at the beach. It is the teacher's responsibility to adapt to the people, not vice versa.

Although risky for the teacher's pride, it is wise to poll the congregation periodically to find out how the teaching is being received. This is not to better "tickle people's ears", but rather to fine tune the style and delivery to best reach the people God has given you to, with God's truth.

2. Good Administration

Most of us have heard of Walt Disney – we grew up with the dream of going to Disneyland. When the story of Disneyland is told, Walt is the hero, the creative genius who, from his imagination, brought dreams to life. Rarely do we hear about his brother Roy. Roy was the guy who made the dreams possible. He was the finance guy, the administrator who took his brother's dreams and made them possible. He negotiated for the land, oversaw the construction, etc. Without organization, great ideas remain nothing more than ideas.

Without good administration churches will never reach their full potential or influence. People will be attracted by the vision and the teaching which supports it, but without administration people will not find their ministry, and hence significance in the realization of the vision.

Every spiritual gift or natural talent is accompanied by its weakness. Administration's weakness is seeing people as little more than resources with which to accomplish the vision.

Highly motivated, type A personalities will have little trouble with being treated as a resource to be used to fulfill a leader's vision, but most people want to be loved for more than what they can do for the vision. They want to be loved for who they are. No one wants to believe that they belong only as long as they are useful.

3. Financial Success

President Calvin Coolidge said, *"...after all, the chief business of the American people is business. They are profoundly concerned with producing, buying, selling, investing and prospering in the world. I am strongly of the opinion that the great majority of people will always find these the moving impulses of our life."*[17]

These words still ring true today. Financial success results in influence in most people's minds. This is true within the church, although hopefully to a lesser degree than in our secular society. We give credibility to those we see as financially successful, even with respect to issues that have nothing to do with the realm in which they made their money. When you think about it, it's kind of crazy – why are we listening to some billionaire giving advice on marriage when he's now on his third marriage? Yet, we find ourselves doing it.

4. Education

All the comments pertaining to financial success apply equally to higher education. For many of us, a PhD after someone's name results in higher credibility and influence. I remember being very impressed with an Anglican vicar PhD while on a ministry trip to England ...until I noticed that he was out of touch with his congregants. He was leading "above their heads".

During our visit I discovered that regarding most of the issues involved with leading a church, he was on no better footing than I was. I must admit though that because of his English accent everything he said sounded credible, until I thought about what he was actually saying. Have you found it to be the case that, almost anything said with an English accent has greater gravitas?

5. Spiritual Giftedness

Christianity is a religion of spiritual power. It is thoroughly supernatural – how could it be otherwise, we are in relationship with a supernatural being. God works His will through us through the power of the Holy Spirit. He does this through spiritual gifts. Some of these spiritual gifts appear to be very much like natural talents which everyone, Christian or otherwise, are born with. This is not the case.

Spiritual gifts are "spiritual" because they are the supernatural works of the Holy Spirit acting through us. The Bible tells us that when we become a Christian, we receive the indwelling of the Holy Spirit and He brings with Him all of His power to accomplish God's will - through us. His power is expressed in what the Bible calls "spiritual gifts."

As I have said, some of these, like administration, teaching, helps, mercy, compassion, etc. appear to be very natural in their manifestations. Others like healing, miracles, words of knowledge, prophecy and tongues have a supernatural character, so much so that they often offend our ability to understand them rationally.

God designed all the gifts of the Holy Spirit to have influence in our lives and in the lives of others. It is largely through spiritual gifts that He interacts with our world. We should expect that the more supernatural the gift the greater the influence. God has set eternity in the heart of man and we find the supernatural intriguing, both for good and for evil. Our present popular culture is obsessed with the supernatural in its worst expressions.

Within much of the church today the supernatural spiritual gifts bring instant credibility and influence. Sadly, just like financial success often results in credibility being given to the wealthy in areas that have nothing to do with making money, often the gift of healing will result in credibility being extended to the healer in areas that have nothing to do with healing.

In our book Reluctantly Supernatural in an Age of Reason, Bob Maddux and I discuss a case in which an accurate prophetic gift resulted in credibility being given to the prophet's attempt to offer an end-times teaching which was not supportable theologically.

Just because someone is an accurate prophet does not make him or her a good theologian, yet how can you fail to take seriously the end-times predictions of a total stranger who just told you what you wrote in your prayer journal yesterday?

Many churches have been built on one or more of the supernatural spiritual gifts. The supernatural always draws a crowd. The question is can that gift alone keep the crowd in the church long enough to transform it into a family of disciples? The answer is usually, "not unless there are more than just the supernatural gifts being employed."

In the Pentecostal/Charismatic movement there has been a confusion between power and holiness. The presence of power has been used as an excuse for the lack of holy character in leadership. Power without character is influential for a time, but without character, lasting influence cannot be maintained.

The same is true for all the sources of influence under our heading of competence. Competence without character has a short shelf life. Erwin McManus puts it well:

"While your talent may have a ceiling, your character does not."[18] Erwin R. McManus, pastor Mosaic church, LA

Know what you lack

Another word about competence; no leader is competent in all areas. A competent leader knows his own strengths, but more importantly, he also knows his own weaknesses. This is essential in choosing who shall be on his team. A good friend of mine recognized his weakness in addressing conflict in a timely manner so he appointed team leaders who were competent to help him sort out responses to conflict situations. He put it this way, "Leaders who pretend to be competent in all areas lose the trust of others by failing to admit their limits and embracing the vulnerably it takes to ask for help. The image that comes to mind is Moses standing on the hill holding up his hands and staff over the battlefield. He could not maintain this position alone. He needed a leader on each side of him to help him to keep his hands and staff in the air."

My question is, is this image an example of Moses' weakness or strength as a leader? Often, admitting our weakness is our greatest strength.

6. Vision

What we usually mean by "vision" is the ability to envision what the goal will look like before its realization. When this revelation comes from God it propels a level of commitment in the followers which is God-empowered and sufficient to accomplish the goal [with God's help.] When the vision is not from God, and it comes through a charismatic leader, it is a recipe for disaster. Jones Town comes to mind...

Without a goal, church life becomes self-centered. The guiding principle becomes, "What's in it for me?" Godly vision calls us to look beyond ourselves for our fulfillment and significance. It calls us to being "outward focused." A church without a vision is a social club.

All godly leaders have a vision. It is through the sharing of their vision that they gain influence. When vision is the main source of a leader's influence it is the vision that has the influence. This means that as long as the people believe the vision is attainable and that the church is making progress toward the fulfillment of the vision, they will continue to give themselves to the vision. Conversely, when progress is not being made, the people will begin to withdraw their efforts from the vision. As well, many of them will stop believing in their leader's vision, with the result that he loses credibility. When this happens, the vision implodes on itself – more people withdraw their support and so the vision fails more rapidly until it dies.

The failure of a vision can result in the death of a church.

"Hope deferred makes the heart sick, but a longing fulfilled is a tree of life." Proverbs 13:12

Where a leader is basing his influence on the strength of his vision, he is taking a very real risk. People are the stewards of their resources and they have the responsibility before God to spend their time, energy and money on those things they believe God is calling them to support. It is logical and inevitable that when a vision is failing many of them will withdraw their support.

Unless vision is supported by other sources of influence of greater impact to the congregation, the church will flounder.

This does not mean that they leave the church or hate the visionary leader. It just means that they stop taking his vision seriously. At this point the more he "sows the vision" the more they disrespect his leadership. In its most benign form this equates to not taking him

111

seriously [at least with respect to his vision.] If his leadership is founded on the strength of his vision, then he is in danger of losing his followers. Unless vision is supported by other sources of influence of greater impact to the congregation, the church will flounder.

One sad response a visionary leader may make as a vision is dying is to come up with another vision. If the second vision is from God, then this tactic might work. This will depend on whether there are other sources of influence coming from the leader which will lend support to the second try. Without these other sources of influence, the visionary leader will only get a few second tries. For many of us, it is three strikes and you're out.

Obviously, I am arguing for a style of influential leadership that comes from much more than a godly vision. **A godly vision without godly character and godly caring will not sustain itself.** People are inherently practical about what they are looking for in an influential leader – most of them are looking for character and caring before vision.

I am tempted to go on to discuss influence through athletic prowess, artistic success, celebrity, etc. but within the church those discussed above were the one's mentioned in my survey.

Competence and masculinity

Here is a tangent related to the subject of competence that is worth exploring. Although competence is the least important of the three factors contributing to becoming a leader of influence, it is the one which men spend most of their energy pursuing. I believe this is because it is the quickest way to achieving significance in the eyes of the world.

Often in our culture our self-worth is measured by our net-worth, and our net-worth is most often determined by our competence. If men are going to fulfill their godly call to leadership, they must prioritize the development of character and caring ahead of increasing their competence. This issue presents men with a good opportunity to work on their self-awareness.

Since competence was the least important of the three "C's" we can now turn our attention to the more important sources of influence, but first...

Some Questions to Consider:

1. The areas of competence discussed in this chapter are: 1] Good Bible teaching, 2] Good administration, 3] Financial success, 4] Advanced education, 5] Spiritual giftedness, & 6] Compelling vision. Which two of these are most important to you in a leader? Why? Which two are least important? Why?

2. The first disciples upon whom Jesus built His church scored high on few of our six areas of competence [as valued in our present-day church.] What did they score high on? [hint: how did they spend their time? Acts 4:13]

3. Have you been a part of a vision that failed? If so, what was your reaction to the failure of the vision?

Chapter 9 – Integrity, Honesty & Authenticity

Before we turn our attention to a discussion of character, we need to mention two aspects of character that have already been discussed: humility and having a servant's heart. Jesus and Paul both had these character traits to the fullest. They are the foundation of godly character and hence influential leadership. This reminder should be kept in mind as we examine the other aspects of what we summarize as "character."

Character is what results from having a healthy moral compass and following it in all our daily decisions. For Christians this moral compass is the word of God – the principles for living found in the Bible. These principles inform all our relationships, family, neighbors, friends, co-workers, strangers and even enemies. Our principle and foundational relationship is with our creator.

Where does character come from?

Character is the result of spending time with the greatest influencer of all time. Without God's daily influence in a leader's life his character will suffer. As his character suffers so does his leadership.

> **Character is the result of spending time with the greatest influencer of all time.**

Many years ago, I read a leadership book by Stephen Covey, the name of which escapes me, but something he said struck me as significant. He said that in doing his research for the book, he read every book on business management that he could find, going back to the early 1900's. He found that up until the 1970s or there about, integrity and character were stressed as essential qualities for successful leadership.

He said that a shift in focus occurred at about that time, after which the vast majority of books on leadership development centered on leadership techniques, without regard for character.

Character matters

I have placed this chapter before those chapters that deal with what an influential leader does [or should do], because actions without character are little more than an attempt at manipulation. In a moment we will look at an example to clarify this point. It has to do with listening. Later in the book we will study the act of listening as it pertains to acquiring influence in the lives of those we lead. One psychologist has said that for most people, being listened to is synonymous with the experience of being loved.

Listening is merely an expression of love, and love is what people respond to which gives us influence in their lives. Genuine, sincere listening is an act of love and the active ingredient in influence is love. Techniques for active listening can be learned, but unless the listener listens with a heart of love, the speaker will sense the insincerity and read this "listening" as nothing more than a management technique. People have a very refined recognition of being loved. They also have a very refined recognition of insincerity. They can "feel" when love is sincere and when it isn't.

Character is what gives all the techniques of acquiring influence legitimacy.

At the heart of character is integrity.

Integrity

The Merriam-Webster dictionary defines integrity as; "1. Soundness, 2. Adherence to a code of values: utter sincerity, honesty, and candor, 3. Completeness"

The word comes from the root verb "to integrate," meaning; "to form into a whole: unite."

Conceptually, integrity involves all the constituent parts of a person coming into unity to accomplish a given action.

Integrity is what results when:

> a leader's moral compass [conscience] prompts a given action

> o   and his or her heart [emotions],
> o   mind [attitudes and thoughts]
> o   and will [choice]

> join in unity to accomplish the action.

At this point the whole person is integrated [united] in bringing about the right action.

What might this look like?

It is easy to see how a lack of integrity could occur in the act of listening:

Your boss calls you into his office. He or she has just read an article about influential leadership through listening. He composes himself with a look of concern on his face when he asks you how you are doing. He says that he is concerned about you, "How are you doing? How are things going at home?"

He invites you to tell him how you really feel about your job, your marriage, and your family. You are about to get vulnerable when you realize this is the first time in years that he has asked you about you or your life. You notice that he is sneaking peeks at his watch, then you see the book on the corner of his desk, "Acquiring Influence Through Listening" [the best seller from Mark Cowper-Smith.] Then you see your sales figures on the other corner of his desk... your numbers are down...

"Of course, now I know why he's listening to me! He doesn't care about me; he cares about my sales numbers! He's not listening to me, he wants to "manage" me. What a phony!"

At the risk of belaboring the point, none of the techniques we will discuss will have lasting effect if they are not done with integrity. In our example, it would have had more integrity, and hence more effectiveness, if your boss had simply said, "I want to talk to you because your numbers are down. What's going on in your life?"

Integrity includes honesty

Nothing undermines influence like dishonesty. Relationships thrive on honesty and die because of falsehood. I have done countless hours of marriage counseling and know, from painful experience, that once a spouse has been lied to, the issue is the restoration of trust. Restoration of trust does not come easily, and why should it? "If he's lied to me once how do I know he won't lie to me again?" Broken promises lead to broken relationships.

In a working relationship, a boss that is dishonest does not usually result in the employee leaving, but it does result in an employee who no longer respects his boss.

In a working relationship, a boss that is dishonest does not usually result in the employee leaving, but it does result in an employee who no longer respects his boss. Once respect is lost the employee has only external motivation to compel him to give his boss his best.

External motivation is often not enough to result in an employee's best efforts. The result is that the boss has lost influence in the life of that employee and now has only external motivation [positional authority] to rely on.

I have heard many employees complain about having a hypocrite for a boss. In every case they default to giving less effort to the boss they disrespect. Hypocrisy is simply dishonesty.

I once knew a leader [pastor] who was impatient in listening to the concerns and opinions of his congregants. To bring the discussion to a close he would routinely tell them he agreed with their position.

Of course, they went away happy until they ran across another church member with whom the pastor had "agreed," only to find that the pastor had "agreed" with the opposite side of the argument. Now we have two people disillusioned with their pastor, and for good reason. Sloppiness with the truth is nothing less than lying. God is crystal clear on this point.

"Let your Yes be simply Yes, and your No be simply No; anything more than that comes from the evil one." Matthew 5:37 AMPC

It is noteworthy to see how important honesty is to God. In this verse, intentionally misleading speech is attributed to the work of Satan! This puts an end to the idea that "white lies" are not harmful in our working relationships, or any relationships for that matter.

Integrity includes authenticity

What do I mean by authenticity? The dictionary defines "authentic" as "genuine" or "real." When we use these terms to describe a person, we are giving them one of the highest compliments possible, but what exactly are we describing? For most of us the answer is what you see is what you get. It is a consistency of heart, mind, emotions and action. None of these contradict the others. Although it is somewhat hard to define, we all recognize it when we see it. And it has an immediate effect upon us.

When we are in the presence of someone who is authentic, we find ourselves giving them instant credibility. We find ourselves listening closely to their opinions or advice. We give them influence in our lives without reservations. This is because there is a direct relationship between authenticity and authority.

God is always and only honest. He is incapable of being dishonest or untrue to Himself. There is no shadow of falsehood in Him. He is, by His nature, truth. He is incapable of having a relationship with anyone on anything less than a foundation of complete truth.

What this means for us is that His truth flowing through us [our spiritual authority] is, in part, in proportion to our authenticity. When we are truest to who He made us to be we have the most credibility [spiritual authority/influence] with those we lead. Authenticity brings authority [influence.]

Just be you

The story of David, King Saul and Goliath illustrates this principle. Allow me to summarize it. David is a young man tending his father's sheep. His older brothers are in Israel's army, ready to go into battle against

When we are truest to who He made us to be we have the most credibility [spiritual authority/influence]

the Philistine army. The Philistines are led by a huge and powerful giant – Goliath. Goliath spends his days challenging and insulting King Saul and Israel's army. His tactic has worked; no one in Israel's army is willing to fight him, man to man. As a result, King Saul and his army has been demoralized to the point of paralysis.

David comes to bring his brothers some food and hears the insults of Goliath, as well as Goliath's promise. Goliath has promised that if any Hebrew warrior can defeat him one on one then the Philistines will admit defeat and serve the Hebrews.

David volunteers to fight Goliath and King Saul agrees, giving David his armor to wear.

"Then Saul dressed David in his own tunic. He put a coat of armor on him and a bronze helmet on his head. David fastened on his sword over the tunic and tried walking around, because he was not used to them.

"I cannot go in these," he said to Saul, "because I am not used to them." So, he took them off. Then he took his staff in his hand, chose five smooth stones from the stream, put them in the pouch of his shepherd's bag and, with his sling in his hand, approached the Philistine." 1 Samuel 17:38-40

The rest, as they say, is history. David, using his sling and some stones, killed Goliath and brought victory to his King and nation. What is interesting about the story is that David would not use King Saul's armor or weapons, even though to do so would have been a great honor. David refused to try to be anything other than himself.

God was with David in his victory, but the real question is would David have defeated Goliath if he had fought in King Saul's armor? Most probably not. David was successful because

God was with him, but also because he would not fight in a way that was untrue to who he was.

This relationship between authenticity and authority [influence] holds true in our leadership today.

> *"We have been collaborating on leadership research for thirty-five years and we keep discovering that **credibility is the foundation of leadership**. It's been reinforced so often that we've come to refer to it as the First Law of Leadership: if you don't believe in the messenger, you won't believe the message. People don't follow your technique; they follow you – your message and your embodiment of that message..."*

> *"What they most want is to know who you genuinely are. This is the key for effective servant leaders."*

> *"Don't confuse leadership with talent. And don't confuse leadership with tools and techniques. They are not what earn you the respect and commitment of your people. What earns you their respect in the end is whether you are* you."[19]

James M. Kouzes and Dr. Barry Posner, Finding Your Voice

What does authenticity look like in practice?

I have heard it said that every leader has a life message which informs everything that he says and does as a leader. It is that one thing that finds a way to come out in every sermon.

I have a friend who is all about discipleship. No matter what the conversation, discipleship is going to come up – it's just a matter of time. He lives and breathes discipleship. Somehow every Bible story morphs into a lesson about discipleship.

For me, my life lesson is all about grace – the ridiculous, irrational, undeserved, extravagant, wasteful love of God for me, a person who truly does not deserve it. Living as the object of His inexplicable love has never lost its wonder for me. This book came about because I have heard lots of great sermons on the grace of God, but very few on what leadership under grace should look like. This book is an attempt to answer that very practical question.

What is a leader without a life message? Someone who is inherently unstable – jumping from one ministry trend to the next, imitating the content and style of the mega-church-pastor-du-jour. He is insecure in His identity because He has not discovered who he is in God and what his unique calling is. He is a bundle of talents and gifts without a deep sense of identity and direction. And people can sense this.

An authentic leader is comfortable with himself. He does not change with the situation. He seems to be at ease wherever he is and with whoever he is with. He is steady and secure. More than that, he is comfortable with his weaknesses. He has defined himself by being equally honest about his strengths AND his weaknesses. This is hugely important to authenticity.

Consciously or unconsciously we are all busy defining a version of our "self" which we project to those around us. It is our projection of the person we wish we were - it is our "image." Usually our image is a composite of all our successes. We define our "selves" as the total of all our accomplishments, talents, and spiritual gifts, etc. But this image is incomplete and as such inauthentic. Rarely, if ever, do we include our failures or our flaws, unless we speak of them in the past tense as something we have overcome [which is really just another success.]

The very weakness that we try to hide is what brings us greater influence.

This false projection has two unintended consequences. The first

122

is that it prevents genuine Christian fellowship because it is only half true – I am not bringing all of myself to my relationships, which means that I cannot be fully known. The irony is that the parts of me which need fellowship the most, the deep insecurities and fears, are never reached. The second is that I fail to grow into my God-ordained influence because I am inauthentic. And there is an irony here as well. The very weakness that we try to hide is what brings us greater influence.

> *"People of deep influence don't hide who they are or the struggles they have. In fact, it is precisely because they are honest about their struggles that we can identify with them; it is their commitment to live with authenticity that draws us to them"*[20] T.J. Addington

My life

At present I am over 70 years old and Shell and I lead a thriving group of people in their 20's and early 30's [along with a few oldies like ourselves.] We meet in our home. This is not the demographic mix of generations that small group gurus prescribe for a successful small group. Current logic tells us that it should not work, after all, what do young adults have in common with old people. The short answer is their doubts, fears, insecurities, unmet prayers and unfulfilled dreams.

I have been leading small groups since I became a Christian. It was in a small group that I rediscovered my faith. This present small group is the second best one I have ever been a part of, for one wonderful reason; we share a level of honesty and transparency that I have never experienced before. I lead the group by trying not to lead the

Everyone wants to feel understood and safe with someone who really "gets" them, and the quickest way to that trust is to let them "get" you.

group. I do not come with an agenda for our discussion. I have only one real goal; to be as transparent about my own issues as I can be. We talk about our lives.

I routinely share my fears, doubts, unmet needs and unanswered prayers. My vulnerability should have our kids [Shell and I call them "the kids"] running in a panic saying to themselves, "who are these messed up people?" In fact, the opposite is true. They regularly tell me that my honesty about my own issues draws them to me, because they know I am safe and that I understand their fears, etc.

We share a fellowship unlike anything I have experienced before. It might be counterintuitive, but authenticity in a leader is winsome. It draws people to you because everyone wants to feel understood and safe with someone who really "gets" them, and the quickest way to that trust is to let them "get" you.

What others are saying

Shell stumbled upon some secular research that reached the same conclusion regarding the relationship between transparency, vulnerability, and successful/influential leadership and group performance.[21] Daniel Coyle, the author of the book "Culture Code", was interviewed on a podcast. From the transcript I will paraphrase his conclusions.

He points out that our commonly accepted wisdom is that trust must proceed vulnerability. In other words, if we are going to be vulnerable with one another it will be because we have established trust between us. According to his research the opposite is true. His conclusion is that vulnerability leads to trust and he suggests that vulnerability involves sharing our weaknesses together.

Coyle cites an interview with a navy SEAL commander who said, "the most important four words a leader can say are "I screwed that up."" Coyle says that groups that share their weaknesses become stronger and conversely, groups that hide their weaknesses become weaker.

Perhaps most relevant to our discussion of leadership is his conclusion about the role of the leader in creating a group in which the group members can be vulnerable. He says that it is the role of the leader to be vulnerable first. As an example, he tells of a senior executive in an industry leading company who counsels leaders to send a regular email to those they lead asking them to tell them one thing they want to see their leader continue to do, and one thing they want him to stop doing. This kind of vulnerability creates influence because it creates a safe environment in which group members can be real and ask for help.

More examples from bible times

Strength in a leader does not equate to managing your fears by hiding them, but by having the courage to allow others into your hidden emotional world.

King David had this kind of relationship with his men. He turned his fears and troubles into songs and sang them to them [just read his Psalms of lament.] With those he led, Paul was transparent about his hopes, fears, and deep feelings for them [as well as his frustration with them.] Jesus invited his friends into the depths of his fears the night before He died. Strength in a leader does not equate to managing your fears by hiding them, but by having the courage to allow others into your hidden emotional world. Integrity, honesty, transparency and vulnerability about what makes you "you" are essential to authenticity. But what if you don't really know what is going on inside of you? What if you are a stranger to your own deep emotions, fears, doubts, and weaknesses. Is it really possible to live an "unexamined life?"

The answer is yes, and the problem is described as a lack of "self- awareness." On to the next chapter...but first...

Some Questions to Consider:

1. Can you sense when someone is pretending to care for you? What is your reaction to him?

2. Have you ever sensed that someone is listening to you just to "manage" or manipulate you? How did you react to that?

3. What does being "authentic" mean to you?

4. How do you react to inauthentic people?

5. I wrote that "When we are truest to who God made us to be, we have the most credibility [spiritual authority and influence] with those we lead." Agree or disagree? Why?

6. How could you be more "yourself" with people?
7. Are you willing to share your doubts and fears as well as your successes?

Chapter 10: Self-Awareness

"So, search your hearts every day, my brothers and sisters, and make sure that none of you has evil or unbelief hiding within you. For it will lead you astray and make you unresponsive to the living God." Hebrews 3:12 The Passion Translation (TPT)

Self-awareness is a popular term coming into prominence in leadership literature, both secular and religious. Is it just another trend or does it have a biblical foundation? What do we mean by "self-awareness?"

A life Lesson

Let me start with a story about myself. I grew up in a legalistic church – too many Pharisees and not enough disciples. Too much hypocrisy and not enough authenticity. As well, I grew up with a mother who suffered from mental illness. As a child she was taken from us for weeks at a time to be hospitalized in the psych ward. She attempted suicide when I was 12. I was the one who found her unconscious on her bed, surrounded by pills. Without going into the details, it left me damaged, but not in any ways that I was willing to examine, or even aware of.

At the age of 28 I came back to the Lord and quickly found myself in a position of leadership in a small house group that eventually grew into a church which I co-led. My intelligence and charisma made it possible for me to rely on these strengths to lead, without having to face my inner brokenness. For years I was completely unaware of my brokenness, but I did notice a pattern of behavior that puzzled me.

Whenever anyone began to leave our group, even for a good reason, like moving to another city, I found myself distancing myself from them to the point of outright rejection. I was aware that my behavior was wrong, but I did it anyway, automatically.

I also found myself unable to say no to people, not a healthy no, but an unhealthy yes. This led to burnout, but on I went with my yes's. Finally, I went for counseling, still oblivious to the reason for my ungodly behavior. The counselor listened to my description of the problem behavior and made a simple request – please tell me about rejection in your life. I closed my eyes to think about it and a movie started playing in my mind. I "saw" myself as a child with my mother, being taken away from us. I felt the fear of being abandoned. I saw incidents of rejection and abandonment throughout my childhood and adolescence. I saw the same kind of incidents right through my adulthood until the present moment. I was shocked!

I saw my history as one of rejecting others the moment I believed they would reject me. I was always the first to make rejection "official", so that I would not be the one to be hurt. Reject before you are rejected! Minimize the pain! Be the one in control!

I also realized that my compulsive "yes" was really just a way to prevent being rejected. That one counseling session was the best money I ever spent. I walked away with an understanding of why I react in a way that I do not desire. More than that, I now had an issue to take to my Father God for healing. My prayer became a request to experience His Father's love in a way that would leave me secure in Him, unafraid of being rejected. And that is what happened! My life and my leadership changed.

Self-awareness is many things, but at the center it is the knowledge of how my history has made me the person I am today.

Self-awareness is many things, but at the center it is the knowledge of how my history has made me the person I am today. It is a knowledge of my strengths AND weaknesses, my passion, temperament, dreams, disappointments, and as-yet unhealed brokenness. It is also an understanding of my sin and areas of temptation.

Blind spots

None of us are perfect, we are works in progress. We have attitudes and actions that cause us to fall far short of God's plan for our lives. This leads to living and leading in a way that does not make us happy or bless those around us, as it could. We all admit to this truth, but few of us are willing to take the journey toward self-awareness. **Our reluctance to examine our lives soberly leads to what we call "blind spots."**

> **Our pride is unwilling to entertain a discussion of our weakness because our pride will have to pay for the cost of change.**

Blind spots are those negative attitudes and actions which we choose to ignore. It is what the legal system calls "willful blindness." Beneath willful blindness lies self-deception. Self-deception is our default position. Blind spots serve us because, at the core of the issue, beneath self-deception, is pride. Our pride is unwilling to entertain a discussion of our weakness because our pride will have to pay for the cost of change. It is our human nature not to want to examine our weaknesses. We will do almost anything to avoid the long look inside, and so we welcome blind spots, usually unconsciously.

Have I overstated our reluctance to engage in self-awareness? Perhaps we can answer that question by looking at a very revealing research study.

Psychologists at the universities of Virginia and Harvard conducted a study in which students were required to sit alone and think for 15 minutes.[22] The students were given an option to sitting and thinking. If they preferred, they could avoid the time thinking by giving themselves an unpleasant but safe electric shock. All the students were given a demonstration of the shock prior to agreeing to participate in the study. It was sufficiently unpleasant as to cause all the students to say that they would pay money to avoid the shock.

Two thirds of the men and one quarter of the women chose the shock. One man chose the shock over 100 times! All to avoid the potential of the long look inside.

The test was administered to adult church members and patrons of a farmers market to see if the results found were particular to students. More than 100 people were tested, aged from 18-77 years old. These subjects also reported sitting alone to think as unpleasant. To answer the question you might be thinking, no they were not offered the alternative of the electric shock.

Bringing God into the process

Clearly, our human nature recoils from self-awareness, yet the Bible counsels us to examine our hearts, motives, attitudes and actions.

"For by the grace given me I say to every one of you: Do not think of yourself more highly than you ought, but rather think of yourself with <u>sober judgment</u>, in accordance with the faith God has distributed to each of you." Romans 12:3

God is calling for honest and accurate thought as we think of ourselves. There is no room for blind spots here.

"Search me, God, and know my heart; test me and know my anxious thoughts." Psalms 139:23

Here the writer is inviting God into the process of self-awareness. What is noteworthy is that the writer is not limiting the process of discovery to the revealing of sin. He is asking God to reveal even his anxious thoughts. As well, it is worth noting that the writer is not asking God to know his thoughts for God's sake. God already knows his deepest thoughts. He is asking God to reveal these things to himself. The point is obvious; we cannot fix problems we are not aware of. The first step to every solution is to recognize the problem.

Jesus promises us help in the process of self-awareness:

"To the Jews who had believed him, Jesus said, "If you hold to my teaching, you are really my disciples. Then you will know the truth, and the truth will set you free." John 8:31-32

Jesus is referring to Himself when He refers to knowing the truth, but I think He is promising more than just the knowledge of Himself. The freedom He is promising must be more than just the freedom from sin. It must also include freedom from self-deception and the destructive blind spots that thwart our obedience to Him. In another passage, He promises us the help of the Holy Spirit to lead us into "all truth."

"But when he, the Spirit of truth, comes, he will guide you into all the truth. He will not speak on his own; he will speak only what he hears, and he will tell you what is yet to come." John 16:13

Of course, Jesus is telling His disciples that the Holy Spirit will tell them of things to come, but when He uses the term "all the truth" He is not just referring to future events. He is promising that His spirit will tell them everything they need to know to live lives that glorify Him. "All truth" must include the knowledge of what must change in our self-awareness to live lives pleasing to God.

Danger zone

I anticipate at this point that some readers may be saying, "this self-awareness sounds a lot like self-focus and introspection, which are often destructive. What's the difference?" Good question. Introspection for its own sake is just self-focus for the sake of self. Self-awareness, on the other hand, is the effort to understand our "selves" for the sake of living and leading more productive lives for God, free from the crippling lies and blind spots that sabotage that effort. It is self-awareness for the sake of Christ-awareness. Self-awareness is the solution to self-delusion, and self-delusion is the enemy of truth.

Self-awareness is the solution to self-delusion, and self-delusion is the enemy of truth.

The Bible counsel's honest self-awareness, but what do secular sources say about self-awareness? Do they agree or disagree?

At the date of writing this book the latest and probably best secular study of self-awareness was done by Tasha Eurich and her associates, entitled What Self-Awareness Really Is (and How to Cultivate It.) Again, I will paraphrase her findings as reported by the Harvard Business Review, Jan 2018.[23]

A number of years ago her team did a large scientific study of self-awareness involving almost 5,000 participants. The goal was to determine what self-awareness is and how to increase it.

As a result of their research they divided self-awareness into two categories: internal self-awareness and external self-awareness. She describes internal self-awareness as *"how clearly we see our own values, passions, aspirations, fit with our environment, reactions (including thoughts, feelings, behaviors, strengths, and weaknesses), and impact on others."*

There was a correlation between internal self-awareness and satisfaction with one's job, relationships, self-control, and happiness in general. The self-aware, as well, suffer less anxiety, stress and depression.

External self-awareness involves how others see us in terms of the same factors. Her research showed that those with higher external self -awareness are more empathetic toward others. As well they are more open minded. They have better relationships with those they lead and are seen by them as more effective leaders. Obviously, it does matter what people think   of   those   who   lead.

It has always been my belief that, with some exceptions, we Christians are responsible, not just for how we see ourselves, but for how others see us. To be oblivious to how we affect others is simply a lack of consideration for them – it is a lack of love. Eurich's findings support this conclusion with respect to the second category of external self-awareness.

It is interesting to note the benefits to the first category of internal self-awareness; freedom from anxiety, stress and depression. This certainly sounds like the kind of freedom Jesus promises. Although it is not the peace that knowing Him brings, it is the peace that knowing the truth about oneself can bring. It is the result of God's common grace to all humans – the grace of knowing the truth about ourselves. The simple truth is you can't fix what you can't see.

Does being internally self-aware lead to being externally self-aware?

One would think that having an accurate self-awareness would lead to having an accurate understanding of how the people in your life see you. Eurich's study found no correlation between the two. Just because you know yourself accurately does not mean you are aware of how others see you:

> *"When it comes to internal and external self-awareness, it's tempting to value one over the other. But leaders must actively work on both seeing themselves clearly and getting feedback to understand how others see them. The highly self-aware people we interviewed were actively focused on balancing the scale."*[24]

The question arises; "how big a deal is a lack of external self-awareness? This effort sounds like a lot of work. Are the benefits worth the effort?" This is a very good question given the fact that the research indicates that only 10-15% of those tested, who believed they were self-aware, actually were. This only confirms our earlier conclusion that self-deception [or at best self-ignorance] is our human default position. Is the work worth the effort?

The answer depends on how important your relationships are to you. Good relationships require good communication, and good communication requires knowing how your words are being received. If your listener believes you are an angry critical person, then your words of affirmation or praise are going to be received as false or manipulative. Likewise, if your listener believes you are a driven and results orientated leader, then your attempts to show care for them by asking them how they are doing at home will be rebuffed as insincere. In all of these examples good communication suffers.

Does this apply to family relationships?

Let's leave the employment universe for a moment and look at family relationships, in particular, parenting. Here is one teen's story:

Sara's (not her real name) father vented regularly about his co-workers' failures and incompetence - in front of her. She experienced his anger and frustration vicariously. Not surprisingly, she reached the conclusion that he is a critical and angry person with unattainably high standards. When he addressed her failure to do her homework, she heard his words as coming from a critical and angry spirit. Her reaction was to protect herself from him emotionally. She began avoiding him until she could not stand to be in the same room with him.

He believed that he was speaking from love [speaking only for her own good], but she believed he was speaking from anger. This was the end of their communication, which only caused him to react with more anger and judgement. The father/child relationship, which was once a source of joy for both of them, became a relational graveyard.

All of life's important relationships suffer when we lack either internal or external self-awareness. The truth is, to speak your mind you must first know your heart. What I mean by this is that communication is not merely choosing the right words to accurately express your thoughts. There is an emotional component to communication that is often more important than the words chosen.

The right words expressed with the wrong emotion results in miscommunication.

The right words expressed with the wrong emotion result in miscommunication. Sadly, many of us fail to take note of the emotion underlying our words. When we do this, we become externally un-self-aware. We are unaware of how we are being perceived. **To communicate accurately and effectively we must know how our words will be received.**

Communicating your thoughts is only half of communication. When we know how our words will be received [how we are coming across] we can tailor our words to best be understood and received by our listener.

If people think of you as an angry person, they will reject your words unconsciously in an effort to protect themselves from a negative emotional attack. They will often do so no matter how true your words actually are. In an effort to protect themselves from powerful negative emotions, they will end up rejecting what might be positive powerful truth. This is why emotional self-control is so important to becoming a person of influence [to be discussed in a later chapter.]

Let's return to Eurich's research to visit two more important findings.

Experience and power hinder self-awareness

According to Eurich, job experience and a position of power tend to convince a leader that he need not question his assumptions or examine evidence which calls his perspective into question. This false security discourages the honest self-appraisal that self-awareness requires. It also encourages us to see ourselves as more self-aware than we actually are. She cites a statistic that only 10-15% of those leaders studied who considered themselves to be self-aware actually were. This is a shocking level of self-ignorance at best and self-delusion at worst.

As would be expected, she also found that the more power the leader holds the more they overestimate their abilities. This is really a pride problem coming to light. It makes perfect sense; senior leaders have few leaders above them to bring constructive criticism, As well, they have few people below them with the courage or foolhardiness to bring uninvited though accurate criticism. Business professor James O'Toole put it well when he said,

"As one's power grows, one's willingness to listen shrinks..."[24]

The solution of course is to invite constructive criticism. And it works. Eurich found that the most effective leaders seek regular critical feedback, with the result that they are seen as more effective leaders, that is to say leaders of greater influence.

"Likewise, in our interviews, we found that <u>people who improved their external self-awareness did so by seeking out feedback from loving critics — that is, people who have their best interests in mind and are willing to tell them the truth.</u> To ensure they don't overreact or overcorrect based on one person's opinion, they also gut-check difficult or surprising feedback with others."[25]

Eurich's conclusions, which I have underlined, are clear evidence of our earlier conclusion that those leaders who operate principally from positional authority are likely to fail to succeed as effective leaders. As we found in our Old Testament review of positional leaders, those who would not listen to their wise counselors ended up as failures. King Saul is a perfect example of how positional power and unfettered authority can result in a leader who, as time went on, became less and less willing to listen to those wise critics God had given him. The irony is that the more Saul consolidated his positional authority, the more he needed to listen to his constructive critics.

To be self-aware we must be willing to listen to those who have the courage and love to tell us the truth about our blind spots. This is true for all of us, but especially for those in positional authority. A positional leader can easily get away with rejecting constructive criticism. He is in a position of power which, by its mere existence, dissuades constructive critics from speaking. The fact is, the more power a leader has the more he or she will have to invite constructive criticism, and **this invitation must include the promise of the leader's best efforts not to react defensively or with anger.**

Very few employees, teenage children, wives or dependent family members will risk speaking the truth to the person who holds their well-being in his or her hands, even when invited to do so. Where the person holding the power reacts with anger &/or defensiveness, the intelligent constructive critic will rarely try it again. Anger and defensiveness are nothing more than a clear statement saying, "I am not open to hearing what you have to say! Don't try this again!" It is the emotional equivalent to the Old Testament practice of "killing the messenger."

> **To be self-aware we must be willing to listen to those who have the courage and love to tell us the truth about our blind spots.**

Earlier in this book we learned of Michael Dell's use of a model bulldozer on his desk to remind himself of his propensity to fail to listen to those he was paying to speak to him. This was a wonderful way in which to remind himself to listen well to whatever his "counselors" have to say to him.

A good leader will remind himself frequently of the need to **invite** constructive criticism, and to **respond with self-control**. Easier said than done, but the effort [even when not entirely successful] will not be lost on those who are trying to "speak the truth in love."

Given the self-control it takes to hear a critic out, it is not surprising to hear the following argument repeated regularly: "I don't need to listen to people in order to be corrected. I have a good relationship with God. He can tell me anything I need to know." I have heard this rationalization many times, almost always coming from the lips of someone who rarely receives correction well. Is it truth or just an excuse for failing to listen well?

God speaks to us regularly about the things that need to change in us, but most of the time He does it through those around us.

The Bible tells us to correct one another, and it tells us how to do it. Jesus tells us to examine the "log in our own eye before we attempt to take the splinter out of another's eye." He doesn't say, "don't ever attempt to correct one another." He is telling us to look at our own failures first before we bring correction to someone else. He is stressing the necessity of an attitude of humility before we speak, and this humility is essential. The fact is God speaks to us regularly about the things that need to change in us, but most of the time He does it through those around us.

It is at this point that "familiarity breeds contempt" comes into play. Those most qualified to bring accurate constructive criticism to us are those closet to us. In a family it would be the spouse or the children, or a brother or sister. In the corporate world it would be a personal assistant, junior executive or fellow board member. Sadly, these are the people whose opinions we most often ignore. Why? Because we are close to them and we have begun to take them for granted. I am continually confounded by the lengths to which humans will go to avoid dealing with their blind spots. Most of the time pride or a fragile self-image is our greatest enemy.

The Solution

My advice is simple but painful; find someone who is close enough to you to make a fair judgement about you, and who has your best interests at heart. Invite them to speak their negative observations to you routinely. Make a commitment in advance to do your best not to be defensive. Take what they say and be as honest as you can about finding the truth in what they have said.

Finally, make it a goal to change the negative behavior you have agreed is true. Ask them to gently point it out to you when they see it happening.

Is this pain worth the effort? Yes, if you do this you will find that you are beginning to like the new you better than the old one, and so will everyone else. You will also become a person of greater influence.

Some Questions to Consider:

1. How would you define self-awareness?" Why is it important?

2. How would you define "external self-awareness?" Why is it important?

3. How is internal self-awareness related to being authentic?

4. In your own words, explain my statement, "to speak your mind you must first know your heart."

5. What would be the effect in your life of inviting constructive criticism from someone close enough to know you, who has your best interests in mind?

Chapter 11: Emotional Intelligence

"EQ" or Emotional Intelligence is one of the latest buzz phrases surfacing in the secular management literature. I am always suspicious of technical jargon. Too often it is the creation of a self-proclaimed expert trying to be original at the expense of clear communication. My first question when confronted with EQ was, what is the definition of the term? Here is what I found in the Wikipedia dictionary.

> *"Emotional intelligence (EI), Emotional leadership (EL), Emotional quotient (EQ) and Emotional Intelligence Quotient (EIQ), is the capability of individuals to recognize their own emotions and those of others, discern between different feelings and label them appropriately, use emotional information to guide thinking and behavior, and manage and/or adjust emotions to adapt to environments or achieve one's goal(s)."*

That's a mouthful, but basically, it's awareness both of our emotions and the emotions of others. In addition, it is using that information to inform our perspective and ultimately our behavior.

The term gained popularity in the 1995 book "Emotional Intelligence" by Daniel Goleman.

Goleman explains,

> "John Mayer and Peter Salovey invented the whole field," when they were chatting about politics while painting a house." Salovey (now President of Yale University) and Mayer (now Professor at University of New Hampshire) were talking about their research on cognition and emotion and got to discussing a politician.

They wondered: How could someone so smart act so dumb? Their conclusion: Smart decision-making requires more than the intellect as measured by traditional IQ."
https://www.6seconds.org/2005/01/30/goleman-emotional-intelligence/

EQ is self-awareness as it applies to emotions; one's own and the emotions of others.

Obviously, EQ has a lot to do with Self-Awareness. EQ is self-awareness as it applies to emotions; one's own and the emotions of others. Another way of describing it is "emotional maturity." A few years ago, I read a great book by Peter Scazzero entitled, Emotionally Healthy Spirituality. His message can be summarized very simply: spiritual maturity and emotional maturity are related. You can be no more spiritually mature than you are emotionally mature.

Emotions matter

Emotional maturity is a contributor to influence because emotions are as important to our sense of well-being as our rational thoughts – for many of us, more important. Think about it – most of the time when you ask someone how they are doing; they reply with a statement of their emotional state; "I feel great!" "I feel sad." "I feel like I am spinning my wheels..." We usually define our present state of being emotionally.

I have already said that communication has as much to do with our emotional state when we speak, as with the actual words we use. "I love you" spoken in anger is a contradiction which rarely communicates love. At the risk of repetition, "to speak your mind, you must first know your

To speak your mind, you must first know your heart.

heart." This makes sense as we examine our own communication, but a high EQ means that we also understand the emotions of the person with whom we are relating. High EQ means being empathetic.

A conversation with a drunk

Most of us have had the experience of being drawn into a conversation with a drunk. We soon realize that we are not communicating effectively. We end the conversation as smoothly and quickly as possible because we know he is not able to receive what we are trying to say. The alcohol has impaired his ability to assimilate our words. Could the same be said of a person overcome with anger or fear or sorrow? I think so. Understanding the emotional state of our listener is essential to effective communication and effective communication is essential to being influential.

Understanding the emotional state of our listener in the moment of our communication is not the only goal. As a result of their temperament, current stresses, successes or failures, our listener brings to the conversation an emotional "default climate", either negative or positive. High EQ means recognizing this emotional climate and adjusting our communication accordingly. This is just a very intellectual way of describing "being sensitive."

High EQ people are sensitive to the emotions of others. This is because they are "others-centered." They enter a conversation with a desire to know how the other person is doing emotionally. They read the clues and respond accordingly. They do not do this with the goal of manipulating the other person, but rather with the goal of understanding the other person at a deep level. People who do this routinely become people of great influence.

143

What my dad taught me

Allow me to tell you how I came to acquire a high EQ long before the term was first coined. All through my elementary and junior high school years I was the smallest kid in my grade. I was not athletic. I was not good looking. I did not have money. I certainly was not a part of any "in crowd." And I desperately wanted to belong.

In my first year of high school I found myself in the home room class of the coolest guy in the school. He was athletic, rich, and popular. He was a drummer in a local surfer band. He dated the leader of the cheer leading team [a genuine babe!] and he had a 1957 powder blue Chevy with a blueprinted 327 engine, a Hurst 4 speed on the floor and tuck and roll upholstery. He was "the man." I wanted to be his friend more than anything!

I told my father how much I wanted to be Bob's friend, but I had no idea how to do it. My father gave me some great advice. He said, "everyone likes to talk about themselves, get him talking about himself and really listen to him."

It sounded crazy, but I did it and it worked. I thought he had this perfect life, but I soon found out it wasn't so. He had real issues just like me. I soon found myself caring for him, not for what I could get out of the relationship [belonging and social position] but for what I could give him as a friend. The friendship passed, as most high school friendships do, but the lesson in listening and empathy is with me to this day.

Our perfect Father is vested in healing our negative conditioned responses that sabotage our relationships and our influence.

Behind empathy is a desire to truly understand who this person sitting in front of me is. What does she think, what is he feeling, what matters to her, what is he afraid of, what are her dreams, etc. I think of it as being an emotional detective. And these are the same questions I ask of myself regarding my own emotions. This is emotional intelligence as it relates to others, but understanding my own emotional climate is equally important.

When I understand the cause or source of my negative emotions I can begin to "manage" them. Managing our negative emotions is largely a matter of bringing them to God to listen to Him in order to understand why I feel the way I do in situations which "trigger" them. Our perfect Father is invested in healing our negative conditioned responses that sabotage our relationships and our influence. He will lead us to the truth about why we do the negative things we do and show us the truth that we need to know to be rid of these responses. Until complete freedom comes, He will also give us His Spirit of self-control to manage our negative emotions so as to protect our relationships and our influence.

The theological way of saying this is to say that emotional intelligence involves the sanctification of our emotions. It is the gradual transformation of our emotional climate through the supernatural influence of the Holy Spirit living within our inner emotional world.

It is sad that so often we see the Christian life as largely a process of behavior modification. Until our emotional life is transformed our actions will be, at best, a result of our willpower, which is exhausting. This is not the emotional healing that our Father desires for us.

Much of what I have said so far is conceptual. Perhaps some examples of low EQ would be helpful for us to understand what it looks like in action.

A lesson from the TV

There was an American sitcom, My Three Sons, which aired from 1960 through 1972. The show was about the life of widower and aeronautical engineer Steven Douglas (beloved actor Fred MacMurray) as he raised his three sons.

In the later years of the show one of the sons, "Chip," was in his first year of college and dating a cute little gal named Polly. The series expanded to include Polly's father, Mr. Williams. The contrast between Steve Douglas and Mr. Williams was comical and certainly demonstrated the difference between low and high EQ.

Mr. Williams parented from a completely different paradigm than Steve. He was suspicious, fearful, controlling, and self-centered. He bounced between angry outbursts and the silent treatment. Let's look at the four categories of EQ:

Self-awareness: Recognizing your own emotional responses to interactions. Understanding how your strengths and weaknesses affect your thoughts and behavior.

Mr. Williams rarely listened to anyone as he was solely focused on his agenda. His fear of losing his daughter clouded every action and word he spoke, but he was not aware of his fear. From time to time someone would challenge his actions and attitude toward the young couple, but he would quickly dismiss the challenge and return to statements such as: "I am the head of this home." [he defaulted to positional leadership]

Steve, on the other hand, was confident regarding the way he had raised Chip and was not fearful. Steve was aware of his irritation with Polly's dad. Everyone in Chip's family could not stand Mr. Williams and although Steve rarely said a negative word about anyone or any situation, he would often say, "I just don't like that man." Steve was self-aware and yet chose not to act out his feelings.

Self-management: Managing your emotions in healthy ways to control impulsive feelings and behaviors and quickly adapt to changing circumstances.

The angry outbursts of Mr. Williams were comical when contrasted with Steve Douglas's calm demeanor. Mr. Williams was a "hot-head." Everyone in the family (including Steve) commented that there was "just something they didn't like" about Polly's dad. Mr. Williams was oblivious to this dislike. Even though Steve didn't like how Mr. Williams was treating the young couple, he continued to listen and respond with quiet thoughtful statements. On the other hand, Polly's dad resorted to manipulative tactics to try to get people to listen and agree with him, creating further distance in all his relationships.

When Chip came to his dad about the idea of eloping, Steve listened well and asked a few financial questions which were helpful. By not losing his "cool" Steve retained influence for more conversations to come.

High EQ - Social awareness: Understanding the emotions, needs, and concerns of other people, identifying emotional cues from others and diagnosing group or organizational dynamics.

Mr. Williams barged into the Douglas home at all hours of the day and night (even in his bathrobe on a few occasions). occasions). He was completely oblivious to common courtesies and was constantly asking Steve to "do something" about Chip pursuing this relationship with his daughter. He would constantly say, "Wouldn't you agree Steve?" That left Steve in his gentle, stuttering replies to say, in fact, that he didn't agree and that the kids would find their own way.

In the dialogues between Mr. Williams, his daughter and wife, the women would often dissolve into tears while Mr. Williams just kept on talking. He was oblivious to the emotional state of his family, and he insisted he was right in his perspectives and decisions and had no need to change.

Relationship management: High EQ people develop and maintain good relationships through clear communication. As well, they inspire and influence others to have positive, clear interactions, to work well in a team and build bonds with others, and to manage conflict in a healthy manner.

In every confrontational conversation Mr. Williams would react so defensively that the conversation would end abruptly. In contrast, Steve would make a comment about the need to stay open to the choices the young people were making. He chose to trust them. Mr. Williams would storm out of the room saying, "*I know what's best for my daughter. She is my daughter.*" [A truth his daughter came to regret]

Mr. Williams did not understand how his insecurity was affecting all his relationships. He maintained his "heavy-handed approach." In one very comical episode Mr. William had Chip and Polly followed by a private detective. The young people were quite scared and asked Steve to talk to the man in the car in front of the house. Steve calmly confronted the man who was sitting in a car outside and found out the whole story. Mr. Williams remained convinced it was the necessary thing to do in this world of constant danger. His cynicism and mistrust toward others drove both Mrs. Williams and Polly away from him, providing Chip with the "final straw." The couple eloped shortly thereafter.

Mr. Williams had driven everyone away through his lack of self-awareness, his inability to manage his emotions and his lack of sensitivity. [low EQ] In contrast, everyone in Steve's family sought him out for advice. Polly's dad was a father without influence, while Steve continued to provide guidance and wisdom to the young couple.

As in most TV family dramas there is a happy ending. In the end, Mr. Williams mellowed out and came to accept both the marriage and his new son-in-law. Steve Douglas' secure, stable, open and flexible traits slowly won over a very difficult Mr. Williams.

Why include a fictional TV drama as an example in this book? Because, both my wife and I have seen just these kinds of "Mr. Williams" failures repeated in more families than we can count. Sadly, the "Mr. Douglas" successes are far too infrequent, but everyone can learn how to increase their EQ. Read on...

Self-awareness and Insecurity

We have already discussed the importance of self-awareness in the previous chapter. One of the consequences of lack of self-awareness is insecurity. A leader who is not aware of his fears and uncertainties is insecure. In his book, "Deep Influence," T.J. Addington writes:

> Insecure leaders are responsible for much leadership disfunction, while personal security – being comfortable with who we are and how God made us – is the foundation for healthy leadership.

> The symptoms of insecurity are many: defensive attitudes, a need to be right, a desire for control, anger when things don't go our way, marginalization of those who don't agree with us, a spirit of criticism, a felt need to be liked rather than respected,

Leaders who cannot control their anger find themselves constantly dealing with staff turnover.

and an inability to differ with others while staying connected.[27]

Self-regulation and Anger

"There is no more destructive tendency among leaders than a short temper."[31]

I grew up with a father who had a bad temper. We walked on eggshells. The moment he came home from work the family was on edge. His anger ruled him and our household. I wonder today how many of my anxieties and insecurities came from living under the constant threat of anger.

Anger, like defensiveness, sends a clear message that says, "I will not be questioned, only obeyed," but it is much more powerful than defensiveness. Anger elicits the fight or flight response in all of us, and usually it is the flight response. We run from relationships infected with anger. Leaders who cannot control their anger find themselves constantly dealing with staff turnover.

Many years ago, I knew a very gifted leader who had a serious problem with anger. He was one of the most gifted leaders I have ever known. His gift mix was amazing. People were drawn to him and responded to his gifting wholeheartedly... until his anger was released, then they left. It is one of the saddest wastes of spiritual gifts I have ever seen.

As expected, the Bible gives us good counsel as to what to do about an angry person. [or leader]

"Do not make friends with a hot-tempered person, do not associate with one easily angered," Proverbs 22:24

Addington gives us 4 questions we should ask ourselves when we are tempted with anger.

1. First, do I have my facts right? Wise individuals know that secondhand information is often faulty. They also know that there are two or more sides to every story.

2. Second, is there another explanation for what I have heard or observed?

3. Third, have I talked to the individual myself to attempt resolution?

4. Fourth, Have I contributed in any way to the failure of the relationship?[32]

Wisdom indeed.

Self-regulation and defensiveness

Defensiveness is another symptom of insecurity and lack of self-regulation. In my experience it is the most destructive response to insecurity. We have already discussed the need for everyone, leader or otherwise, to have those people in their lives who will point out their blind spots and weaknesses. We don't grow without constructive criticism. A defensive response to constructive criticism is really saying, "don't do this and don't try this again." It also says, "I am not interested in what you have to say." It takes a very strong person to persevere with constructive criticism in the face of defensiveness. Most people just decide to clam up and let the person fail, leaving his growth to the school of hard knocks.

Ironically, in adopting a defensive posture, leaders actually lose credibility with others, even though they feel they have preserved it by defending their position. **Defensive leaders live with the illusion that they know what people think, when in reality their defensiveness leaves them clueless and deeply vulnerable.**

As we have already seen, being wrong in our belief about what others think of us concerns the second half of self-awareness. Unfortunately, being defensive when criticized is our human default position. Pride [the root of all sin] demands a defensive response. For this reason, cultivating an intentional attitude of openness is essential. The quickest way to openness is to pre-empt the auto-defensive response by being proactive and inviting constructive criticism. By doing so we can pre-condition ourselves to hearing something negative and to responding with "tell me more" or "please give me an example", rather than being defensive. Hard work, but worth the effort.

> *Healthy leaders work constantly on developing an open, rather than defensive, persona. They do this by first controlling the natural tendency toward defensive reactions when others disagree with or criticize their position. Rather than going defensive, they ask questions and make reflective statements like, "If I hear you right, you are saying..." or "Unpack that for me so that I better understand what you are saying."[28]*

Social awareness

A few years ago, I did some research on Narcissism. I found that it is now considered a mental illness. It is essentially, extreme self-focus or self-centeredness. All of the authorities I researched reached the conclusion that it is incurable. It is at the extreme of a spectrum that all of us are on. At one end is humility and at the other is narcissism. We are all susceptible to self-centeredness and yet we can all choose humility. The Bible tells us to humble ourselves, so we know it is a choice we are empowered by God to make.

Although self-centeredness is our default position by virtue of our human nature, we do not have to be ruled by it. The problem for positional leaders is that their position as leader makes self-centeredness natural and easy. The antidote has already been discussed – cultivating a habit of inviting constructive criticism and reacting to it without defensiveness.

It is noteworthy to see the psychologists' conclusion about narcissism being incurable, aligning with Addington's advice to those working for a narcissistic leader.

"I am sometimes asked by staff members what to do if they work for a narcissistic leader. Generally, I suggest they leave."[30]

Strong words indeed, but perhaps an accurate indication of the depth of the problem of narcissism.

Relationship management and Micro-management

Insecure leaders feel a need to control others while secure leaders set boundaries within which they release staff to use their gifts and wiring to accomplish the task.[29]

One of the clearest signs of an insecure controlling leader is micromanagement. Micromanagement may be necessary in the early phase of training a new leader, in fact, it usually is. The problem arises when it persists beyond its "expiration date." It is most destructive when the leader imposes his or her personal preference on a matter which has been delegated to the junior leader - where the choice is merely as to a matter of personal opinion or taste.

Micromanagement is often simply an insult. It says, "I do not trust your judgement on minor matters of style or taste. My choice is better. I am your boss, so do what I say." This is the death of creativity because it reduces the junior leader to nothing more than an appliance or functionary of the boss. It is profoundly demotivating. I was in a position of leadership years ago in which I was given responsibility without authority. It felt like being given the keys to a delivery van, without gas in the tank. It results in pure frustration.

Micromanagement communicates distrust on the part of the leader. Distrust by the leader breeds distrust in the follower. No one gives their best to a leader they do not trust.

Although our present discussion is focused on leadership in the workplace, we need to remind ourselves that all the principals of increased influence apply equally to all our relationships, family, friendships, neighbors, marriage, acquaintances and co-workers.

How does God lead us?

God seems much more interested in what I learn from my mistakes than in preventing them.

One of my guiding principles for developing influential leadership is to use our Father God's example of how He leads us. When I look back at my development as a leader, I find that God has been the ultimate non-micromanager with me. I am amazed at the mistakes He allowed me to make and continues to allow me to make. He does not seem to be embarrassed by my failures. God seems much more interested in what I learn from my mistakes than in preventing them. If this is how He leads us, how can we choose to lead otherwise?

What do I do with the consequences of my God-given freedom to fail – my negative emotions and responses?

When I understand the cause or source of my negative emotions I can begin to "manage" them, and by managing them I am not talking about stuffing them down and trying to ignore them. Our negative emotions and inappropriate responses are trying to tell us something. They are the red lights on the dashboards of our lives. The red

Our perfect Father is vested in healing our negative conditioned responses that sabotage our relationships and our influence.

154

light on the dashboard is not the problem. It is merely an indicator of a deeper problem somewhere else in the car. It is a messenger. So, what do we do with the message?

Managing, understanding, and responding to our negative emotions is largely a matter of bringing them to God to listen to Him, in order to understand why I feel the way I do in the situations which "trigger" them.

Our perfect Father is invested in healing our negative conditioned responses that sabotage our relationships and our influence. He will lead us to the truth about why we do the negative things we do and show us the truth that we need to know to be rid of these responses. Until complete freedom comes, He will also give us His Spirit of self-control to manage our negative emotions so as to protect our relationships and our influence.

Some Questions to Consider:

1. How would you define Emotional Intelligence?

2. Why is it important?

3. How do you respond to an angry person?

4. Have you ever been micromanaged? If so, how did you respond to it?

5. Have you ever been given responsibility without authority? What was the result? What affect did it have on you?

6. What do you think of Addington's advice to someone who is working for a narcissistic leader ["Generally, I suggest they leave"]?

7. Have you ever taken your negative emotions to God and asked Him why you feel the way you do, and when that reaction started? If so, what did He show you?

Chapter 12: Leading by Example and Teachable Moments

Leading by example was the most common character trait mentioned in the survey I did to determine the source of influential leadership. It is a mark of integrity in the leader, and it inspires followership. Closely related to it was the related answer, "he does not ask me to do anything he is not willing to do himself."

Both of these are signs of humility. They are the evidence of humility in action. Both speak volumes about the character of the leader. We see both in the life of Jesus.

Jesus

As Jesus is the best leader who has ever lived it would be wise to study his model of leadership development. Jesus set out a process for discipleship/leadership development that has never been improved upon. Here is a quick summary of His model.

1. He called them to Himself – not to a religion but to a **relationship**. Christians are not called to something; they are called to someone.

"As Jesus went on from there, he saw a man named Matthew sitting at the tax collector's booth. "Follow me," he told him, and Matthew got up and followed him." Matthew 9:9

Jesus called His followers to a three-year camping trip. He welcomed them into His life **before** He called them into His vision. They became inseparable for a 24/7 three-year relationship. If a leader is going to have great influence, he is going to have to share himself with those who follow him. Jesus is stressing the importance of relationships first, vision second.

A leader who relies on the power of his vision will find himself alone when the vision is frustrated, and the followers are disillusioned. Where the relationship to the leader is relational first and visionary second, the followers will have a reason to remain beyond the draw of the vision.

2. He shares His purpose. [vision]

"Come, follow me," Jesus said, "and I will send you out to fish for people." Matthew 4:19

A leader without a vision is not a leader, he is a maintenance man. The community now formed must have a goal.

3. He takes them with Him while He does ministry, and they watch how He does it. He leads by example.

"Jesus went throughout Galilee, teaching in their synagogues, proclaiming the good news of the kingdom, and healing every disease and sickness among the people." Matthew 4:23

Jesus begins by doing the work that His followers will ultimately do, but He does it first. He begins by **leading by example**. They learn by watching Him.

4. He uses **teachable moments** from their life together to train them for the ministry they will soon be responsible for. His teaching method is **not theoretical but practical**. Because they are sharing life together, daily life provides the opportunities for Jesus to use teachable moments.

"When they came to the crowd, a man approached Jesus and knelt before him. "Lord, have mercy on my son," he said. "He has seizures and is suffering greatly. He often

falls into the fire or into the water. I brought him to your disciples, but they could not heal him." "You unbelieving and perverse generation," Jesus replied, "how long shall I stay with you? How long shall I put up with you? Bring the boy here to me." Jesus rebuked the demon, and it came out of the boy, and he was healed at that moment. Then the disciples came to Jesus in private and asked, "Why couldn't we drive it out?" He replied, "Because you have so little faith. Truly I tell you, if you have faith as small as a mustard seed, you can say to this mountain, 'Move from here to there,' and it will move. Nothing will be impossible for you." Matthew 17:14-21

One of Jesus' best teachings about faith arose out of His disciples' first failure to exercise the healing gift. If you examine the teachings Jesus gave to His disciples, you will find that almost all of them arose out of everyday unplanned experiences. Life is the classroom. We can take advantage of teachable moments by taking those we are leading along with us to ministry appointments.

5. He gives them His authority, with responsibility, and sends them out to do Kingdom deeds:

"Jesus called His twelve disciples to him and gave them authority to drive out impure spirits and to heal every disease and sickness... These twelve Jesus sent out with the following instructions: "Do not go among the Gentiles or enter any town of the Samaritans. Go rather to the lost sheep of Israel. As you go, proclaim this message: 'The kingdom of heaven has come near.' Heal the sick, raise the dead, cleanse those who have leprosy, drive out demons. Freely you have received; freely give. "Do not get any gold or silver or copper to take with you in your belts—no bag for the journey or extra shirt or sandals or a staff, for the worker is worth His keep." Matthew 10:1-10

When you give authority without responsibility, you have power without direction, which leads to chaos. When you give responsibility without authority, you have direction without power, which leads to burnout and frustration. Jesus gave them both together, with clear instructions as to how to proceed.

6. He lets them fail and He uses their failure to teach them, e.g. the demonized boy they could not heal. Matthew 17:14-21

7. He watches how they do the ministry, then He critiques them and gives further instructions:

"After this the Lord appointed seventy-two others and sent them two by two ahead of him to every town and place where he was about to go." Luke 10:1

"The seventy-two returned with joy and said, "Lord, even the demons submit to us in your name." He replied, "I saw Satan fall like lightning from heaven. I have given you authority to trample on snakes and scorpions and to overcome all the power of the enemy; nothing will harm you. However, do not rejoice that the spirits submit to you, but rejoice that your names are written in heaven." Luke: 17-20

Brilliant, isn't He?!

What goes into leading by example?

> **Leading by example is an exercise in humility. When a leader leads by example he is saying, "There is no job that is beneath**

Leading by example is an exercise in humility. When a leader leads by example he is saying, "There is no job that is beneath me." He is also sending a clear message that the job he is doing, in leading by example, is as important to the vision as any other job that he

160

routinely does. He is saying to His followers "the work you do is important." **Through leading by example, the leader is imparting worth to those he leads and to their passion, calling and spiritual gifts**. Here is an example you won't see very often.

A successful example

A pastor I knew was faced with the most common problem a church routinely faces – finding enough volunteers to teach in the Children's ministry. [Sunday School for those of us old enough to remember the term] No matter what he said to the congregation, the problem remained the same. His dilemma was finding a way to convey to the church how important teaching their children about God is. His solution was radical but effective – he turned the preaching over to his associates and he taught in the Children's ministry! He did not have to resort to guilt or manipulation. All he had to do was to lead by example, and it worked.

"Invisible" ministries

The Apostle Paul tells us in chapter 12 of 1 Corinthians that there are spiritual gifts that do not receive the honor that they deserve. They are usually the "behind the scenes" ministries. He tells us that these gifts/ministries should be treated with special honor. Leading by example in one of these "invisible" ministries not only speaks to the humility of the leader but also to the goal of honoring the neglected or taken for granted ministries. This increases the leader's influence.

A not so successful example

When a leader fails to lead by example his influence decreases. A friend of mine told me a story of a leader he had many years ago. The senior leader needed some landscaping work in his back yard. The men in the church organized a Saturday workday and started the work in the morning. The leader was at an elders meeting for most of the morning. [doing important spiritual work] When he got home, he went out to see how the work was going.

It was a very hot day, and the workers were tired and hot. We should note that the leader was young and able bodied. He was more than capable of joining in the work but instead he commented on how hot it was and how much he wanted a lemonade. He then disappeared into his house to spend the rest of the day drinking lemonade.

Whether or not he was aware of it, his actions sent a very clear message, "I am more important than you are. Physical work is beneath me. You are the workers; I am the leader. You are here to serve me." My friend lost respect for his pastor and his pastor lost influence in the eyes of many of his followers.

Another very bad example

Here is another sad story. In my friend's own words.

> *"I hired a gifted worship pastor. One day she walked into the church office and told the church secretary to do some copying for her. Our secretary politely explained that the copy machine was running copies for another staff member but if she wanted to leave them with her, she could get to her copies later. Alternatively, if she wanted to go ahead and make her copies right then, she could pause the machine on its current run and do it herself. She looked at her angrily and said, "People like me tell people like you what to do and you do it!" When our secretary reported it to me, I fired her by the end of the month. My comment to our HR committee was that you can't get much farther from Jesus than that."*

Walk the talk

What we are discussing here is best summarized by that familiar expression, "Don't just talk the talk, walk the talk." Mark Miller, from Chick-fil-A, puts it succinctly,

> *"Embody the values. People always watch the leader – whether we want them to or not! They are generally looking for clues regarding what's important to the leader. They are also trying to determine if the leader is trustworthy. So, what's the link between embodying the values and trustworthiness? If a leader says something is important, the people expect that person to live like it's important. The gap between what we say and do as leaders can be lethal. People generally don't follow a leader they don't trust... Leaders must do everything humanly possible to walk the talk!"* [33]

I have seen leaders "sell" an event to their staff and congregation as critically important to the vision of the church, and then not show up to it themselves. The result is that the leader is no longer taken seriously when he announces something as "critically important." Worse, it can also be fatally destructive to the leader's relationship with the junior leader over the ministry being neglected. Nothing is more demotivating than having your passion devalued by your leader. This results in a loss of influence which often cannot be regained. When a leader fails to show up for an important program, event or campaign he is saying that he is special, that his words for everyone else do not apply to himself.

There is a very important distinction to be made between being "special" and being "specialized." Certainly, senior leaders will not have the time to be a part of every outreach or community building program in the church. Their work is specialized, but that fact does not make them special.

Shirk the perks

One of the ways that leaders can avoid the allegation of elitism is to reject some of the perks of positional authority. King David did this intentionally. When he was overcome with thirst and made an offhand comment about desiring a drink of water from a particular source, three of his most loyal men risked their lives life to bring him a drink of that water. When he was presented with the water, he refused to drink it. He was making a gesture of solidarity with his men who could not drink of the same water. He actually poured it on the ground!

Dave Ramsey put it well when he said,

> *"Your team will share your values, so make sure you're modeling what you want them to emulate. That means no executive perks and no ivory towers. Maybe it means eating lunch in the company break room every day and getting your own coffee every morning. If there's an all-hands-on-deck emergency, make sure your hands are on deck too."*[34]

Don't forget to explain why you are doing what you are doing.

Before we leave our discussion of leading by example, I have an example of a failed attempt at leading by example. It comes from Robert the reluctant mega church pastor we met in chapter 2. As the church grew a problem developed with access to the washrooms during the Sunday services – too many users and not enough washrooms. The problem was hardest on the young mothers with toddlers. Robert decided the solution was to encourage the staff and ministry volunteers to use the staff washroom, an inconvenient distance from the sanctuary.

He set out to lead by example. He routinely used the staff washroom, and all of the staff and volunteers became aware of what he was doing. Unfortunately, none of them emulated his example. When a new senior pastor came to the church, he made it a rule for all the staff and volunteers to use the staff bathroom. This led to much grumbling and complaining – he had their obedience but risked losing their hearts.

Robert learned something we can benefit from; when you lead by example, make sure to explain to your team why you are doing what you are doing, then invite them to join you. Once a few join, most of the rest will follow – willingly – for a win/win solution. This becomes what we call a teachable moment.

> **Life has a way of raising profoundly important questions which are best answered in the moment of need.**

Leading through teachable moments

We have already seen Jesus make use of teachable moments in His development of a group of disciples. The fact is most of Jesus' teachings came about through teachable moments. **Life has a way of raising profoundly important questions which are best answered in the moment of need.** It is said that necessity is the mother of invention. It could equally be said of wisdom. Wisdom is best taught and received when it is most needed.

One of the dangers the Western church faces is the over-intellectualization of our Christian faith. We tend to desire to reduce a living faith to a predictable theoretical one. Theology is often divorced from the practical concerns of our daily lives. In many seminaries, pastoral care and theology are taught as separate classes. This is an unfortunate distinction because it is pastoral problems that theology springs from. The book of Romans provides an excellent example.

Life in ancient Rome

The writings of Paul, and in particular the Book of Romans, contain the theology of grace that distinguishes Christianity from all the other world religions. Romans is a theological masterwork, but it cannot be divorced from the circumstances that led to its writing. Allow me to provide the backstory.

Paul is writing to Christians living in Rome. It is not clear how Christians came to be living in Rome. Probably they were Roman Jews who became followers of The Way in Jerusalem on the Day of Pentecost. When they returned to Rome, they established churches of fellow Jewish Christians. In AD 49 the Roman Emperor expelled all the Jews from Rome, including the Jewish Christians. The expulsion eventually lapsed, but in the meantime the Roman Gentile church became the prominent expression of Christianity in the city.

On returning to Rome the Jewish Christians found themselves in an inferior position to the Gentile church. This resulted in a disunity that Paul had to address. The Gentile Christians favored a faith that devalued the Jewish law and traditions, and of course the Jewish Christians wished to preserve as much of their Jewish heritage as possible. Paul, as both a Roman citizen, a Jew, and a follower of Jesus, was the perfect person to grapple with the job of clearly defining the difference between Christianity and Judaism. What we define as Christianity today, and in fact who we are as Christians, is a direct result of a pastoral problem Paul had to face. The Book of Romans was a teachable moment.

The same can be said of First and Second Corinthians. Our theology of church discipline, sexual mores, gender roles, celibacy, the administration of the supernatural gifts of the

166

Holy Spirit within the church and many others, all arose out of pastoral issues. Paul gained great influence through his grappling with real-life church issues. He was at his best as a teacher and theologian when he was using teachable moments to lead the churches he planted.

My father's leadership through teachable moments

My father had a practice of using his children's life experiences as teachable moments. Before I describe his practice, it will help if I tell you that he never led a family Bible study, nor did he ever attempt to teach us the Bible in any organized way.

What he did was use good questions at dinnertime about each of our days at school. I can remember one conversation with great clarity. I was in 4th or 5th grade and I was the smallest kid in my grade. I was bullied regularly. We were eating dinner and my father was doing what he always did, asking us about our day at school.

I told him that we had a new kid in school – a jockey's son. He was the littlest kid I had ever seen in my grade. With great joy I announced that the new kid had taken my place as the littlest kid in our class and now he would be bullied, and I would escape my suffering. I was thrilled!

My father did not seem to share my happiness. He began to question me about what the new kid must be feeling in his new hostile environment. The more questions he asked the more I began to empathize with the new kid. I could feel his pain because it had been mine. My father asked me what a Christian would do in this situation.

It didn't take long for me to reach the conclusion that this kid needed a friend. On my own, without coercion or manipulation, I decided to become this kid's friend. I did and to my surprise the bullying stopped, against both of us! I have never forgotten that lesson and how my father gently led me to the right conclusion.

Our daily lives provided him with teachable moments. These were situations in which we were presented with a decision that was relevant to our faith. Once he found such a moment, he would drill down with questions about what Jesus would do. He would confront us with our bad decisions and let us discover what could have been a Christlike response. He never lectured us, he just forced us to think like a Christian – all through good questions. [which we will discuss in another chapter]

An influential leader will actively look for the circumstances which create teachable moments.

The awareness of teachable moments is not just a corporate concern. An influential leader will be attentive to the life circumstances of the individuals he leads. Their moments of greatest need are his moments for the greatest influence. Influence gained this way is "money in the bank."

Some Questions to Consider:

1. What is the difference between a lesson taught in a classroom versus one learned on the job?

2. Jesus could have used a classroom model to train His disciples but instead He chose to live His ministry with them. Why?

3. Have you ever had a leader who did not practice what he preached? If so, what affect did this have on you?

4. How can you look for "teachable moments" in your leadership?

Chapter 13: Security in the Love of the Father

Insecurity breeds insecurity

Insecurity is like a virus - it is highly contagious. An insecure leader multiplies his insecurity in those he leads. Confidence is contagious too. Confidence in a leader breeds confidence in those he leads. It results in a sense of security that survives difficult circumstances. It brings with it the kind of perseverance that brings breakthroughs. So where does a leader's confidence and personal security come from?

For those who do not know God, security often comes from a combination of natural talents and time. We call it "experience." When we are looking for a guide, we want one who has been to where we want to go. That is the whole point of having a guide. But the question arises; "who guides the guide?" It is here that God enters into the picture.

Jesus' security

We have already looked at the story of Jesus washing the disciples' feet. It was an act of deep humility, some might say "humiliation." Where does this kind of personal security come from? In Jesus' case it came from His relationship with His Father.

"Jesus knew that the Father had put all things under His power, and that he had come from God and was returning to God; so he got up from the meal, took off His outer clothing, and wrapped a towel around His waist. After that, he poured water into a basin and began to wash His disciples' feet,"** John 13:1-17

Jesus knew His identity, worth, and security were tied to His relationship with His Father. Can there be any greater identity than being the creator of the universe's well-loved Son? Think for a moment of the peace this must have brought Him!

Most of us, most of the time, derive our sense of worth and security from the positive opinions of those around us. This is a very insecure security. It is fickle; one day we are a hero and the next we are a scapegoat. It is a rollercoaster ride at best. Anyone who has been a leader for any length of time knows what this ride feels like.

Not so for Jesus. He was not a victim of pride when He was being hailed as the Messiah on His triumphal entry into Jerusalem, and He was not a victim of the fear of failure, shame or insecurity when, a few days later, He was being scorned the night before His death.

We can have the security that Jesus had

What would it be like to lead with this kind of God-empowered security? Is it humanly possible? If so, how do we get it?

Jesus gives us the answer when He taught about the role of the Holy Spirit in our lives.

"But I tell you the truth: It is for your good that I am going away. Unless I go away, the Counselor will not come to you; but if I go, I will send him to you... But when he, the Spirit of truth, comes, he will guide you into all truth. He will not speak on his own; he will speak only what he hears, and he will tell you what is yet to come... He will bring glory to me by taking from what is mine and making it known to you. All that belongs to the Father is mine. That is why I said the Spirit will take from what is mine and make it known to you." John 16:7-14

The important thing to note is that one is coming [the Holy Spirit] who will take what is "of the Father" and given to Jesus, and He will give it to us. All that Jesus receives from the Father is to be given to us! This is undoubtedly one of the greatest promises Jesus makes to us. The questions become.

"What is this thing that is worth Jesus leaving for? What is this new thing that has never been seen before? What is this eternal thing, existing between the Father and Jesus, which is about to be given to us?"

It is something the Holy Spirit does which is a new work, not seen before in human history. The Apostle Paul describes what this "ministry" of the Holy Spirit accomplishes when he contrasts it with the ministry of the Law in the life of the nation of Israel.

"Now if the ministry that brought death, which was engraved in letters on stone, came with glory, so that the Israelites could not look steadily at the face of Moses because of its glory, fading though it was, will not the ministry of the Spirit be even more glorious? If the ministry that condemns men is glorious, how much more glorious is the ministry that <u>brings righteousness</u>! For what was glorious has no glory now in comparison with the surpassing glory. And if what was fading away came with glory, how much greater is the <u>glory of that which lasts</u>! Therefore, since we have such a <u>hope, we are very bold</u>. We are not like Moses, who would put a veil over his face to keep the Israelites from gazing at it while the radiance was fading away... Now the Lord is the Spirit, and where the Spirit of the Lord is, <u>there is freedom</u>. And we, who with unveiled faces all reflect the Lord's glory, are being <u>transformed into his likeness with ever-increasing glory</u>, which comes from the Lord, who is the Spirit." 2 Cor. 3:7-17

The effect of this new work of the Holy Spirit is amazing! It brings righteousness. It comes with a glory that lasts. It brings glory to Jesus. It brings us hope, boldness and freedom. Finally, it transforms us into the likeness of Jesus! What is security and confidence if not boldness and a freedom that lasts? Surely, this is the same source of security that empowered Jesus' life. And it is here for us!

How do we obtain this security?

What is interesting about this passage is that Paul describes all of the effects and benefits of this work of the Holy Spirit, but he does not tell us how the Holy Spirit accomplishes this. To answer that question, we have to look elsewhere in the writings of Paul to find his explanation for how this security is accomplished:

"For you did not receive a spirit that makes you a slave again to fear, but you received the Spirit of sonship. [adoption - childhood] And by him we cry, "Abba, [daddy] Father." The Spirit himself testifies with our spirit that we are God's children." Romans 8:15

"Because you are sons, God sent the Spirit of His Son into our hearts, the Spirit who calls out, "Abba, Father." So, you are no longer a slave, but a son [or daughter]; and since you are a son [or daughter], God has made you also an heir." Gal. 4:6

The thing that God gave to Jesus, which the Holy Spirit gives to us, is the full measure of the love of the Father. When Jesus was being baptized the Holy Spirit came upon Him and God spoke from heaven saying, "This is my son in whom I am well pleased." In this moment Jesus' identity as God's son was confirmed to Him supernaturally.

172

What is enlightening to note about this affirmation of sonship through the Holy Spirit, was that it was given to Jesus **before** he did anything to earn it. [before His ministry began]

God gives us the same affirmation of sonship, not because we have earned it but because He has adopted us into His family, through His Fatherly love. It is not a result of our efforts or worthiness – it is not earned but given. That is why we call it "grace."

There is a security that comes from being a son that no servant, no matter how faithful, will ever have. A servant can fail at being a servant, but a son can never fail at being a son. A servant is secure as long as he is a good servant, but a son is always a son, no matter his successes or failures, and so his identity is secure.

How does God "feel" about you?

The wonderful truth is this; the Father longs to have you as His child. No matter how old you may become, it is His great joy to enjoy you as His child forever. He gave up the life of His son to make you His child. You are His great joy! Really!

The effect of this security

It doesn't take much imagination to realize what a difference it makes in the life of a leader to have the security and identity of being God's well-loved child. That reality is contagious. A leader who lives under that blessing will transmit it without effort. It is the influence of grace. It is not an influence based on what you do, but rather, what you are. It is a

> There is a security that comes from being a son that no servant, no matter how faithful, will ever have. A servant can fail at being a servant, but a son can never fail at being a son.

security based on identity and not on effort. And it is hugely influential.

What is our part?

Perhaps you are wondering how this transformation of identity is received. What is our part in the process? How does a leader co-operate with the Holy Spirit in His ministry of adoption?

We already have a hint from our survey of Old Testament leaders. The successful ones all had what I have called a "conversational relationship with God." We see the same conversational relationship between Jesus and the Father. Jesus, and these leaders, spent significant time in the presence of God. They were "friends of God." They learned to recognize God's voice. They waited upon Him for guidance. They spent time in prayer. They cultivated an internal stillness which made hearing His still, small voice possible.

The simple truth of the matter is that no one is more influential than the one who has spent much time with God. Again, it is an influence of being, not doing. It is a spiritual authority that can be spiritually sensed. The common people said of Jesus, "He is not like the Pharisees, He speaks with authority." The Sanhedrin took note of the courage of Peter and John.

> **The simple truth of the matter is that no one is more influential than the one who has spent much time with God.**

"When they saw the courage of Peter and John and realized that they were unschooled, ordinary men, they were astonished, and they took note that these men had been with Jesus." Acts 4:13

When we spend time with Jesus, we come under His influence and through His influence we are being transformed into His likeness. This likeness includes His influence. We are

174

influenced and become influential. It is a relational reality, and it is available to any person willing to invest time into their relationship with their Father God.

Being with God brings a security that is tangible. It is sensed by those around us, and it brings great influence with it - much greater influence than any other single thing that we can do. Is it time to spend more time with Him?

A new kind of prayer [being, not doing]

If the answer to that question is yes then there is one more matter to consider, and that is the type of time we devote to being with Him. I have talked to many leaders about their prayer times and most of them describe them as some sort of labor. They describe what we refer to as "intercession." They come on behalf of their church. They are standing before the Father asking Him to bless their work for Him. Intercession includes praying for those we lead, for physical healing, healed marriages, family relationships, financial breakthrough, etc.

When this kind of prayer becomes personal it usually includes prayers for wisdom, insight, guidance, inspiration, vision, etc. It is usually focused on doing a better job of being a leader. In other words, it is prayer about the work. It is rarely relational. That is to say, prayer for the purpose of just knowing God as our Father and being with Him for no other reason than to know and enjoy His company. When I have described this kind of relational prayer to leaders, I have been met with blank stares and often the response of "But that kind of prayer isn't accomplishing anything for God. It is a waste of my prayer time which is hard to come by."

Such a response belies the problem; it indicates that time spent with God must be another kind of work about the work. It reduces our relationship with God to that of Master and Servant. It neglects the father/child relationship from which

175

real identity and security come. It also robs God of His opportunity to enjoy us as His children. What father would respond with joy when he calls his child to himself with a desire to hold her close and she responds with, "I am too busy doing my chores, maybe another time."

> **It may be counter-intuitive, but we need to receive His affectionate love <u>before</u> we try to give it away.**

Somewhere in our service to God we must find the time to be with Him for nothing more than allowing Him to express His father's heart to us. It is His desire to do so, and it is our great need to receive His affectionate fatherly love. It is the fuel that fires our service to Him.

It may be counter-intuitive, but we need to receive His affectionate love **before** we try to give it away.

Where do I start?

Here is my advice for how to start; find those passages that have spoken His love to you in the past. Write them down on a sheet of paper. Sit down and get comfortable and then remind yourself that the time you are about to spend **with** Him will have nothing to do with your work **for** Him. Acknowledge that the purpose of your time with Him in these minutes will be solely for the purpose of receiving His Father's love. Read over the scriptures slowly and stop as soon as any word or words touch you with a realization of His love. Consciously pause to allow His love to fill you and don't go back to reading the passage until the experience of His love fades.

If you make this a daily habit, you will soon find your relationship with Him changing, as will your security and sense of self-worth and confidence. And finally, without making it your goal, your influence as a leader will increase. Those you lead will take note that you "have been with Jesus."

On to leading from love, but first ...

Some Questions to Consider:

1. Jesus was both God and a man. His Father spoke intimate words confirming His identity as God's son on the day of His baptism. Did Jesus the man need to hear these words of the Father?

2. If you answered yes to the first question, do you need to hear these words as well? Have you heard your heavenly Father say them to you? If not, why not? If so, when was the last time you heard Him affirm His love to you?

3. I have said that much of the time our prayer life focuses on our work for God and what we need Him to do for or through us. If you were God, would it please you to have your child come to you this way most of the time?

4. How can you change your prayer life to include more time just being with your heavenly Father, just for the sake of the relationship?

5. Where does your security come from? Do you need more?

Chapter 14: Leading from Love

"All you need is love, love is all you need"

The Beatles,
All You Need is Love, 1967

Finally, we arrive at our third and most important characteristic of influential leaders – love. It seems trite to say it, but **love is the most irresistible source of influence.** It is the source of God's influence over our lives [we love Him because He first loved us], and it is the source of our greatest influence in the lives of those whose lives we share. It makes perfect sense - we give our trust to those we believe love us.

What is not trite is understanding the relationship between positional authority and love. Willard Waller the noted American sociologist studied the relationship between power and love. One writer summarized his findings as follows:

"Willard Waller discovered that there seems to be an inverse relationship between love and power. He noted that in interpersonal relationships as love increases, power decreases; and as power decreases, love increases. He coined the term "principle of least interest" to describe the phenomena, revealed by his studies, that power lies in the hands of the person who cares the least about the relationship. Love and power, it seems, cannot coexist, at least in this world." [35]

Influence is love without control - leadership without resorting to positional authority.

Jesus tells us that in the world of humans we will have to choose between God and money, we cannot serve both. He as well tells us, by His example of divesting Himself of His positional authority and taking the role of a servant, that we must choose between power and love. They do not co-exist because power seeks to control, and love seeks to set free. Influence is love without control - leadership without resorting to positional authority.

The characteristics of caring are the characteristics of character in action. Caring is what a leader of high character does, but it comes as an outgrowth of who he is in his relationship with God.

Leading with a father's heart

In the last chapter we saw that remaining in the Father's love results in a personal security that sets a leader free from all of the insecurities that come with leadership. In addition to that, receiving the Father's love results in a leader who has more than enough love to give to those who follow him. You can't give what you are not receiving. **Those who regularly receive love, regularly give love.** One leader I know puts it this way, we are designed by God to give from the overflow of that which we receive.

We can take this truth further and say that the way that we have been loved by God is the way we will love others, particularly those we lead. As we have been Fathered by God, we will father others. As we have been led by God, we will lead others. Because God's leadership comes from a father's heart ours should as well. The practical question becomes, what are the characteristics of a good father?

179

The characteristics of a good father

In their book The Blessing,[36] Gary Smalley and John Trent give the 5 components of the blessing that children need from their father. They are: 1. meaningful touch, 2. a spoken word, 3. attaching "high value" to the child, 4. picturing a specific future for the child being blessed and 5. an active commitment to fulfilling that future.

In the baptism experience of Jesus His father fulfilled the first three of these components. The first blessing that Jesus experienced was the actual touch of His Father, the Holy Spirit descended upon him. This is the experience of the Holy Spirit "coming upon" a person, which is seen frequently in the Old Testament. The experience is almost always transformational. The value of this touch cannot be overestimated by those who have experienced it.

The second blessing that Jesus experienced was the spoken word of God. This is not just a thought that came to him; this is a **real voice** that he experienced. He heard His father say, **"This is my Son, whom I love; with him I am well pleased"** Matt. 3:17 Again, a transformational experience.

The third blessing that Jesus experienced is the "high value" His Father placed upon him. The words spoken communicate three essential things necessary for a father's blessing: 1. I acknowledge your identity – you are my son! 2. You are the object of my loving affection! & 3. You please me! No more affirming words can be spoken.

Smalley and Trent suggest that these three blessings, plus the last two, are essential to a successful father/child relationship. The Bible makes it clear that we should expect to receive these blessings from our Father God in our own relationships with Him. Let's take a moment and see what the Bible tells us about our Father God's love for us:

1. Meaningful Touch.

"For you did not receive a spirit that makes you a slave again to fear, but you received the Spirit of sonship. And by him we cry, "Abba Father." The Spirit himself <u>testifies with our spirit</u> that we are God's children." Rom. 8:15

Of this passage Martyn Lloyd Jones wrote, *"It is important that we should be clear about the nature and the character of this proof: and I am emphasizing this particular point because I find that many of the commentaries really miss it altogether. But what we have here is not something that is deducted from the truth stated in verse 14, not merely another way of saying that we are led by the Spirit: it goes well beyond this statement. This is something subjective, something which essentially belongs to the realm of feeling and subjectivity, and the emotions. It is something within us at a deeper level than the level of the intellect. That seems to me to be the vital point in this statement. What the Apostle is emphasizing here is that not only must we believe this doctrine, and accept it with our minds, but we must also be conscious of it, and feel it: there must be the Spirit of Adoption in us as a result of this work of the Holy Spirit. Paul is really telling us that we are to feel – and I am emphasizing feeling – in this sense, what our Lord Himself felt."*[37]

God's touch

This experience is what many accurately describe as a "touch" from God. It is an experience of the love of God, not just an idea about God's fatherly love. It is a profoundly meaningful experience. It is difficult to exaggerate its importance because most of the time we lead the way we have been led. This truth deserves a full explanation.

For most of us, we adopt our model of fatherhood from our earthly father. We do this unconsciously and naturally. What this means is that if we were raised by a harsh, critical father

181

we will usually lead in a similar way – we assume that this is the right way to do it. After all, it is the only model of fathering [leadership] that we have known. Conversely, if our father was patient, kind and merciful, we will usually lead from these traits. In either case, the important point to note is that we do this unconsciously – it comes naturally. Because it comes naturally, we do not question our style of leadership.

Our "natural" leadership style remains unconscious until we come to "know" God. **At this point most of us begin to see the nature of God as our Father through the lens of our earthly father**. We do this even though the Bible accurately portrays God as a perfect father. The Bible tells us that God is the perfect balance between justice and mercy, love and discipline, work and rest, etc. Still, we interpret these truths through the filter of our earthly experience of being fathered, resulting in a skewed understanding of our heavenly Father. We then lead/father in a manner consistent with our skewed understanding of the fatherhood of God, and we do it with a "biblical justification" for our skewed leadership, because we can find examples of God's discipline and even anger in the Bible. Isn't self-deception annoying?

It is at this point that we begin to see the value of self-awareness. Real self-awareness comes because we begin to ask ourselves questions about how we came to act the way we do, feel what we feel, and think the way we do. It questions our basic assumptions of how we see ourselves. In this example we ask ourselves, "why do I lead the way I do?" "How has my relationship with my earthly father affected how I lead?" "How does my leadership style compare to that of Jesus or the Father?" "Is my present leadership style fully Biblical?" "What biblical leadership principles and examples am I ignoring?"

Theological self-awareness

Usually our self-awareness is focused on our "self" and hence is psychological in nature, but there is another area of self-awareness that is of greater importance. It is our theological self-awareness. Theological self-awareness concerns our understanding of the nature and character of God as our Father. As I have already said, we usually wrongly define it through our experience of how we were fathered by our earthly fathers.

At the risk of redundancy, let me repeat that we do this even though the Bible contradicts our errors in understanding. This is because we read the Bible through the lens of our experience. Obviously, this is a trap.

The solution to escaping this trap is a change in our experience of being fathered. This is the work of the Holy Spirit. Once He touches us with the supernatural love of our Father God our paradigm must change. This is what happened for me. It was the transformational experience of my life. It changed everything, my self-awareness, my theological awareness, my awareness of the value of others, and my leadership.

In my case I changed from a leader under legalism to a leader under grace. Once we have experienced the love of the Father we can begin to lead with the love of the Father. For those who want to explore this transformation I suggest you read my book, "Is God Religious?" See mark.cowpersmith.org

Below is an example of a leader's life and workplace being transformed by the experience of the Father's love. This is coming from my friend Les, in his own words.

"I was a very left-brained (logical) thinker most of my life. An attorney by trade, who had a senior management role with eight people reporting up to me. I was a fair person, but I was

considered difficult to get to know because I was "all business." After 10 years on my job, the Holy Spirit began working on my heart in church to seek Him more. I had been a Christian for 25 years at that time, but I really did not feel love for many people outside of my own family. At work, I recognized that social time and personal recognition were important to most people, but for me the priority was getting the work out on time and without mistakes.

Realistically, I saw people as tools to get the work done. I encouraged the members of my team who liked to celebrate birthdays and other "mile markers" to do so, because I was not one to remember to celebrate or care about setting up such events.

It is difficult to describe how it feels when God is pursuing you, but my wife and I both hit a point in our evangelical church where we said, "is this it?" Was sitting in the pews on Sundays all that God had for us? We began seeking the Lord and asking what more we could do. We began seeking out speakers and churches walking with the Holy Spirit and moving in spiritual gifts. As God touched my heart, I began praying daily for Him to fill me with His love so that I could love other people more. I knew I did not love others enough, and that I could not represent Jesus Christ on earth if I did not love others.

Within a few months of these daily prayers, I felt a real internal desire to ask my workers how they were doing, to open time in each meeting to chat with them, and to seek to encourage them more often. I began attending the celebrations and taking time to write them each a personal email on their special occasion. After about six months of treating employees "like Jesus would treat them" one of my trusted employees asked me privately if I was sick or dying. When I said I was not sick, she said "It sure seems like you have changed who you are in the way you treat everybody- almost like you are dying and being nice to everybody *on the way out!" She encouraged me "to keep up the good work," and I testified that my heart change was the result of meeting the Lord in relationship and "keeping up His good works."*

Following this Holy Spirit-enabled desire to see my employees as people and to care more about them, I found it was easier to trust them with projects rather than just being a task master. I was able to delegate more work to them, which gave them a bigger picture of the Company dynamics and they appreciated being bigger role players rather than project stewards.

My employees treated me with more respect too, rather than just cursory greetings and needs-based telephone calls. We became more solid as a team, and often joked about "why are you being so nice - are you dying?" We also noticed that when employees trust they are safe to raise new ideas or complaints, full discussion typically leads to new solutions and the employees feel more empowered to do a better job."

It is the Father's desire to lavish His fatherly love upon us, and it is the work of the Holy Spirit to make it real to us. Our part in this process is to desire it, seek it, and trust Him for it.

2. A Spoken Word

Jesus said, **"My sheep listen to my voice; I know them, and they follow me."** [John 10:27] The Bible is full of examples of people having a conversational relationship with God. We should expect to hear His thoughts on a regular basis. Our faith is a relationship rather than a religion and the heart of any relationship is communication.

> Our faith is a relationship rather than a religion and the heart of any relationship is communication.

As I have previously said, the best way I have found to hear His thoughts is to have a notebook and pen available while I pray.

185

As I pray and ask Him questions, I pause regularly and listen [pay attention to] the thoughts that come to my mind. I write them down, leave them for a week or two, and then return to read them again. It is wonderful for me to realize how often He has "spoken" to me. I cannot imagine living without receiving His thoughts.

"A spoken word" means much more than issuing commands and instructions in order to accomplish the task at hand. It means making a real interpersonal connection with those being led. It means having time to talk about more than the job. It means asking the kinds of questions that show a genuine interest in the life of the person being led. It means having the desire, and taking the time, to really listen to the one being led. [as will be discussed in a later chapter]

3. Attaching "high value" to the child

"Can a mother forget the baby at her breast and have no compassion on the child she has borne? Though she may forget, I will not forget you! See, I have engraved you on the palms of my hands..." Isaiah 49:15-16

This and countless other scriptures tell us of the immeasurably high value our heavenly father places upon us - the cross being the ultimate expression of our value to Him.

"Attaching high value" to the one being led means actively looking for things to praise in the follower. It means celebrating their successes equally with your own. It is an attitude that says, "Your success is my success." It means focusing on their successes more than their failures. It means keeping praise as the leader's default position, and criticism as the exception.

4. Picturing a Specific Future for the Child being Blessed

"For I know the plans I have for you," declares the LORD, "plans to prosper you and not to harm you, plans to give you hope and a future." Jer. 29:11

"Picturing a specific future" for the one being led means seeing their potential and "speaking it into them." It means being relentless in affirming their possibilities. It means regularly reminding them of their potential. It is saying "I believe in you" in every possible way. It means seeing their future and speaking it into their present.

5. An active commitment to fulfilling the blessing

"...he who began a good work in you will carry it on to completion until the day of Christ Jesus." Phil. 1:6

"I am not focused on your present weaknesses as much as I am on your developing strengths."

Being "actively committed to the fulfillment of their future potential" means doing all that can be done to see them become all that they can be. It values what they can become more than what they are accomplishing now. It is saying, "I am not focused on your present weaknesses as much as I am on your developing strengths." It is a commitment to doing whatever can be done to see the one led become all that he can become, no matter the cost to the leader. A good father desires that his child will succeed far beyond his success and he is committed to that success.

The Apostle Paul saw himself as a father to those he led. [1 Cor. 4:15] An influential leader will bring the heart of a father to those he leads. He or she will bring meaningful touch to those they lead. This does not mean physical touch, but rather the touch of loving concern for those being led. We will discuss this loving concern in a later chapter.

187

We have just described the way Jesus led and leads us. He is our prime example of leadership from the heart of a perfect father. He is considered by secular historians to be the most influential person who ever lived. If we make leading like Jesus our goal, we will grow in our love and influence with those God has given us to love and lead.

Later we will return to His example as we explore more of what leadership from love looks like in practice.

Leading with the heart of a friend

Jesus redefined His relationship with His disciples with one word.

"I no longer call you servants, because a servant does not know his master's business. Instead, I have called you <u>friends</u>, for everything that I learned from my Father I have made known to you." John 15:15

It is significant that Jesus decided to call His disciples "friends", but it is even more significant that He did so after ceasing to call them servants. He is clearly drawing a distinction between being a servant and being a friend. It is possible to draw the conclusion from His statement that being a servant and being a friend are incompatible. At the very least, Jesus is implying that being a friend is far superior to being a servant.

The basis for Jesus' friendship with His disciples is His transparency with them concerning His relationship with His father, "everything that I learned from my Father I have made known to you." He has kept no secrets from them, his heart is an open book. He is honest about what is most valuable to Him –His relationship with His father.

A friend of mine recently retired from pastoral ministry. He was a pastor of a local church for decades. Once retired he was welcomed into the circle of my friends. The other day he told one of them that it is wonderful to finally have a group of friends to belong to. I am happy and sad for him. Happy because he finally has a circle of good friends, but sad because he went without that for so many years.

When I was a young pastor, I was told by older church leaders not to make friends with the people in my church. They told me I would get hurt. The same advice could have been given to Jesus, and it would have been true. He came to His own and they rejected Him, and yet He still chose to call His servants "friends." I did not take the advice given because I could not imagine serving and leading people, I could not consider my friends.

Truth be told, I did get hurt and I was rejected by some, but those that remained were the means of my healing. Jesus risked friendship with his followers and most of them abandoned Him at the cross, yet He still treated them as friends.

What is a true friend?

I have given much thought to the ways God has been my friend because I want to give that kind of friendship to those I lead. Here are some of the characteristics that define a friend for me.

1. Someone with whom you have no secrets.

The deeper the honesty, the deeper the friendship. A friend is someone you can go to about anything. A friend is someone you feel safe with.

2. Someone who receives you, accepts you and listens to you while suspending judgement. The key phrase here is "suspending judgement." If we are not sure of being accepted without judgement, we will not share the broken and sinful parts of ourselves that are in need of a friend's listening ear.

3. Someone who listens without judging, **yet who still tells you the truth you need to hear.** This is what it means "to suspend judgement." A friend does not ignore our sin or brokenness, but "suspends it" in order to establish acceptance **before** speaking the truth that hurts but heals.

4. Someone whose only motive for "judging" or speaking the hard truth, is healing. This is easy to agree with and very hard to practice. Within each of us is a Pharisee fighting to get out. Without the love of unconditional acceptance, truth is a weapon. The only thing that makes the truth tolerable to hear is pre-existing love. A true friend is always motivated by love.

5. Someone who only, and always, wants the best for you. A true friend will choose your welfare over his own.

6. Someone you can trust with your life.

I trust God as my friend because He has been all of these things for me. He has great influence in my life because this is who He has been for me. As we emulate His friendship with us with those we lead, we will find our influence rising, without a conscious effort to create it.

All of the foregoing six points came from my prayer journal as thoughts I accepted as from Him. He told me we were friends and I asked Him what a friend is. Those were what I heard and took as His answer. It was clear to me that He was my friend, but I wondered how I was His friend. I asked Him, "How am I your friend?" This is what I believe He said,

"You come to me first on every major issue. You care most about what matters to me. You want to hear what I think. You want to please me - that is how you want the best for me. You care about my reputation. You want people to know how wonderful I am. You obey what I tell you to do."

190

It strikes me that as a leader these are the responses, I would most want from those I lead. If we lead as a friend, we should expect those we lead to respond to us as friends. Working with friends is far more satisfying than working with servants. The risks are worth the rewards.

My comments about being a friend to those we lead could be construed to suggest that by being a friend we relinquish our positional authority to lead. This is not true, nor is it what I am saying. As will be discussed later, none of what we do to lead through influence requires that we abdicate our position of authority.

Being in charge means having to make decisions that are not always supportive of the friendships we have with those we lead. This is part of the cost of leadership. The point I am making is that if we have treated our followers as friends, they will usually be much more understanding of the unpleasant decisions we have to make.

A Biblical example

In bringing correction to the Corinthian church Paul said this.

"For I wrote you out of great distress and anguish of heart and with many tears, not to grieve you but to let you know the depth of my love for you." 2 Cor. 2:4

In bringing correction to the church Paul was speaking as the positional leader over the Corinthian Church, but by describing his distress, anguish and tears, he is speaking as a father and as a friend. He is also revealing the depth of his love for those he is correcting. It is more than possible to be both boss and friend at the same time. It is more time consuming and requires more effort, but the equity earned as a friend pays dividends when hard decisions must be made.

A contemporary example of the power of friendship

I want to close this chapter with a story from my early years as a pastor.

Suzie came to our church from the street. She had abused drugs and suffered all of the degradation that accompanies life on the street. She was a total mess; no self-worth, hearing self-destructive voices in her head, subject to radical mood swings, etc. She called herself a Christian, but she had grown up in a very legalistic church. We began counseling. I was relatively confident in my own experience of the love of the Father, so I believed it was just a matter of time before she experienced her own touch of His love and left her brokenness behind.

Two years of regular counseling passed without discernable improvement. I was at my wits' end. I had tried all the techniques I knew, and I had failed her as a counselor. I decided I had to end our counseling sessions. I was unhappy with the decision because I had failed her, but more than that, I had begun to see her as my friend, and I was sorry to see our friendship end.

I remember the phone call clearly. I intended to tell her I could no longer be her counselor because I had nothing left to give, but what came out of my mouth surprised me. I said, "I am not doing you any real good as a counselor, but I like you and want to have you as my friend. Some of us are going down to a blues club to listen to music this weekend, how about you come and hang out with us?"

She came in her new identity as my friend. She began to improve from that day forward. She met a great guy in our church and married him. Today she is the mother of great children and a happily married woman. Friendship accomplished something that counseling could not, because counseling says, "you are important to me because you are my client" but friendship says, "you are important to me because you are my friend." Friendship imparts worth and that is why friends are influential.

Some Questions to Consider:

1. I have said that you cannot give what you are not receiving. Does this apply to our love for others? If so, how are you going to get more love to give?

2. I have said that as we have been fathered by God, we will father others. How have you experienced God as your father?

3. Smalley and Trent's 5 components of a father's blessing are: 1. meaningful touch, 2. a spoken word, 3. attaching "high value" to the child, 4. picturing a specific future for the child being blessed and 5. an active commitment to fulfilling the blessing. Which of these have you experienced from God? Which do you need most? Which do you have the most difficulty giving to those you lead?

4. I have said that as we have been led by God, we will lead others. How has God led you?

5. Theological self-awareness is the awareness of how our life experience [principally how we were fathered] has shaped how we "see" God. Why is theological self-awareness important? Are you theologically self-aware?

6.
    Have you experienced God as your friend? How would knowing Him as a friend change how you see Him? How would it change your relationship with Him?

Chapter 15: Asking Good Questions

What does asking good questions have to do with being an influential leader? It seems counterintuitive – good leaders provide good answers, so why waste time asking questions? Good question. [pun intended]

Early in my leadership development I noticed that people apply the truths they arrive at themselves more often and more thoroughly than those they receive from others. Most people learn by trial and error rather than by taking the advice of others. [even those who are much wiser and more experienced] Most of us have had the experience of telling a child something like, "Don't touch the stove!", only to hear the cry of pain when the child learned the lesson the hard way.

What is influence?

The definition of "influence" is "the act or power of producing an effect without apparent force or direct authority." Telling someone how to do their job or live their life, when stated by one in leadership, is an act of direct authority. Asking a good question that prompts that person to analyze the issue for themselves and arrive at their own answer is indirect. There is no apparent use of force, but more than that, the answer they arrive at is one that they "own." Because they own it, it has a much greater likelihood of being applied.

So, what if they reach the wrong conclusion? Ask another question that leads them in the right direction.

When you ask a person a question, they become vested in trying to answer it. They become connected to the question in a much deeper way than they do when hearing a statement. Questions are engaging. They challenge us. They provoke us to think. Leading through questions brings the person into the problem in a way that brings the best of them to the problem.

Author David Hoffeld, [CEO and chief sales trainer at Hoffeld Group, a research-based sales training, coaching, and consulting firm] has summarized the research questioning the neuroscience behind the brain's activity when responding to a question:

"Questions trigger a mental reflex known as "instinctive elaboration." When a question is posed, it takes over the brain's thought process. And when your brain is thinking about the answer to a question, it can't contemplate anything else."[38]

"When your brain is thinking about the answer to a question, it can't contemplate anything else."

Clearly, asking a question involves much more of the person than what is involved when you simply tell them the answer – they become engaged and focused upon the question. The question, in effect, demands the brain to provide an answer.

Hoffman cites research that revealed that simply asking a person if they were going to buy a new car within the next 6 months increased the likelihood of them buying one by 35%! Questions are powerful motivators!

Asking a question also affirms the value of the person being asked. It is a way of saying, "I believe what you have to say matters... you matter." Research has shown that questions which involve asking a person their opinion activates the pleasure center of their brain. Asking someone their opinion bestows value upon them.[39]

Another story about Mark and his father

Being asked a question by my father became a rite of passage which I will never forget. I was 26 years old and had lived all my life as his son. It was always clear to me that as far as my identity was concerned, in his eyes I was his son, and certainly not his equal. One afternoon he asked me to sit outside with him, because he had something to talk to me about. I suspected it was the usual - I had done something wrong. It turned out he was in a situation which he was unclear about. He told me he wanted my opinion. I was shocked. Nothing like this had ever happened before. I felt an immediate sense of increased self-worth.

He took some time setting out the facts of the situation and then he asked me what I thought had happened; was he in fact "used" by his "friend" or had he misunderstood or misread the facts? I broke down the facts as I understood them and told him as far as I was concerned his friend was no friend at all, and yes, he had been used.

He thanked me for my time and opinion and then I got up to go back inside the house. As I placed my hand on the door handle to open the door, I had an epiphany – "He just treated me as an equal. I am no longer just his son. I am now his friend as well." This moment changed our relationship, and we were close friends until the day of his death. Asking questions imparts worth.

Before we drill down into how to lead through good questions there is another significant benefit to asking good questions. It has to do with self-awareness and emotional intelligence. By asking good questions we "coach" those we lead into greater self-awareness. We have already discussed the value of self-awareness in a

You can't help someone to be the best they can be if you don't know who they are to begin with.

leader, but it is of equal value in those we lead. The more they understand themselves accurately the easier they are to lead.

The same applies to emotional intelligence. The more the leader understands the follower's goals, dreams, fears, strengths and weaknesses, the more he can direct that person toward success. Asking good questions and paying close attention to the answers brings the leader to a place of genuine understanding of the inner landscape of the follower. This understanding makes bringing the best out of the follower much easier. **You can't help someone to be the best they can be if you don't know who they are to begin with.** Good questions provide this knowledge.

Good leaders lead through good questions and so it should come as no surprise to us that Jesus asked a lot of questions.

Jesus' questions

The four gospels record Jesus asking 175 questions. As well, He often answered questions with a question. In my Bible the 4 gospels cover 116 pages. This means an average of 1.5 questions by Jesus per page. When we consider that much of the gospels are in narrative form, the ratio of Jesus' questions per page compared to His non-question teaching is much higher. Jesus was the master of leading through questions – great probing, revealing questions. Here is a sample of them:

1. What do you want?

Jesus began his mentorship of His disciples with a simple question; **"What do you want?"** [John 1:38]

He often performed a miraculous healing after asking the question, **"What do you want me to do for you?"** This is a reasonable question to ask when you don't know what the problem is, but Jesus often asked this question when the problem was obvious. In one instance 2 blind men were begging by the side of the road. As Jesus passed by, they called out for mercy. He responded with the "What do you want..." question. [Matt. 20:32]

In a similar instance a blind man called out for healing and Jesus asked him the same question. The blind beggar answered "Lord, I want to see!" Jesus responded to him, "Receive your sight; your faith has healed you." Jesus could have healed the man without asking him the obvious question but, by asking the question the blind man was provoked to exercise his faith. His response is a response of faith – he calls Jesus "Lord." [Luke 18:41]

The word "lord" used here comes from the root "to have power or authority." The blind man was exercising faith in Jesus and Jesus responded with a display of His healing power and authority over blindness.

2. Do you want to get well?

One of the most interesting questions Jesus asked occurred at the pool of Bethesda in Jerusalem. This was a place of miraculous healing for the blind, lame, and paralyzed. It was customary for the sick to lie by the pool and wait for an angel to stir the water. The first person into the water was healed. There was an invalid man at the pool who had been waiting 38 years for his healing! When Jesus learned of how long he had been waiting He asked him, "Do you want to get well?"

Coming from anyone other than Jesus this seems like a strange and pointless question, even cruel. Why else would he have waited at the pool day and night for 38 years? The brilliance of the question is apparent to anyone who has been chronically ill for a long time. It is equally apparent to those who have shared life with a chronically ill person.

As a means of coping we adjust to being ill. We accommodate ourselves to being "a sick person." Eventually the illness becomes a part of our lives, even a part of our identity.

Think about this man at the pool. For 38 years being at the pool has been his life. His food is brought to him by others. He has not had to work for 38 years! The pool is his life. Perhaps he sees his identity as a sick person. Perhaps he is not ready for the radical changes that being healed would bring. Perhaps there is a part of him that would rather not accept these changes. Perhaps he has not considered this question for decades. Now, Jesus confronts him with the most relevant question of his life; **"Do you want to get well?"** John 5:1-6 The question is an invitation to self-awareness.

3. Who do you say I am?

Who we believe Jesus to be is the most important question we can ask and answer. He came as God in human form to reveal the nature of God to the world. In order to entrust His message and ministry to his disciples He had to know they knew His true identity. Naturally, we assume that He would make His divinity clear through repeating the message endlessly, after all, the disciples were not the sharpest knives in the drawer. This is not the case. Most of the time he left it to His disciples to connect the dots.

He did this by starting with a simple question. He asked them, **"who do people say I am?"** They replied, **"Some say John the Baptist; others say Elijah; and still others, one of the prophets."** Jesus followed with another question; **"But what about you? Who do you say I am?"** Peter got it right when he said, **"You are the Christ."** [Mark 8:27-29]

This is an example of allowing a person to reach a correct conclusion without forcing it upon him. A conclusion we arrive

199

at by ourselves is far more important and persuasive than one we receive passively.

Another very powerful example of this kind of questioning occurred shortly after Jesus preached His most controversial and misunderstood message. While teaching at the synagogue in Capernaum, Jesus said **"I tell you the truth, unless you eat the flesh of the Son of Man and drink His blood, you have no life in you. Whoever eats my flesh and drinks my blood has eternal life..."**

Many of Jesus' disciples reacted predictably saying, **"This is a hard teaching. Who can accept it?"** Worse, many of His disciples turned back and no longer followed Him. If ever there was a time to be direct about the meaning of His words, this was it, but Jesus chose the indirect approach. He led with a question. Addressing His 12 original disciples he asked, **"You do not want to leave too, do you?"** Peter responded for all of them by saying, **"Lord, to whom shall we go? You have the words of eternal life. We believe and know that you are the Holy One of God."** [John 6:53-69]

Peter gave the correct answer, but more importantly he arrived at it on his own. Jesus could very well have said, "You should not leave because I have the words of eternal life. You need to believe that I am the Holy One of God." This would have been the most direct way of ensuring that they believed correctly, and it is the way most of us go about dispensing the truth, but is it the best way to teach? Because Peter arrived at the truth by himself, he believed in it more deeply, and so it meant more to him.

> A good leader gains influence when he gives ownership of the problem to his team, rather than simply issuing a command to solve it.

4. What are we going to do about this problem?

Jesus used questions to test His disciples' faith and to bring them into the problem-solving process. On one occasion Jesus had a genuine problem on His hands. Jesus sat down on a mountainside to teach. A crowd of thousands gathered. Jesus had no source of food to feed the huge crowd and so He asked Phillip, **"Where shall we buy bread for all these people to eat?"** The question was a test for Phillip – did he believe Jesus could feed all these people. Phillip's answer is perfectly rational – **"Eight months wages would not buy enough bread for each one to have a bite!"**

Because Jesus included Phillip in the problem by asking him his opinion, Phillip will experience the miracle that Jesus is about to do, more personally. It will be more glorious to him because he was burdened with the problem. He had a vested interest in the solution. [John 6:1-7]

A good leader gains influence when he gives ownership of the problem to his team, rather than simply issuing a command to solve it.

5. Where are your accusers?

The Pharisees [a compassionless lot] catch a woman in the act of adultery. The offense is punishable by death by stoning. They have no interest in the fate of the woman. She is just a stage prop they will use to trap Jesus. The Mosaic law requires that she be killed, yet they know that Jesus is beloved by the people because of His mercy and kindness. It is the perfect trap. If Jesus upholds the law, then He is lacking in mercy. If He gives mercy, then He is soft on sin and disrespects the law. Either way they win.

Jesus' answer is brilliant. He says, **"If any one of you is without sin, let him be the first to throw a stone at her."**

This has the desired effect and slowly the crowd of legalists leaves. When they are all gone Jesus asks her a simple question; **"Woman, where are they? Has no one condemned you?"** **"No one, sir."** And Jesus said. **"Then neither do I condemn you."**

Why did he ask her where her accusers were? He could just have said, "I don't accuse you either, now go and sin no more." By asking her the question He is compelling her to take note of what has happened. The reality is that she no longer has any accusers. The truth is there for her to see – they are gone. Jesus has used a question to bring home the truth to her, through an object lesson.

Many times, I have counseled those who live under the belief that they are unlovable. They wear glasses of shame and they see rejection where it doesn't exist. I can tell them the truth that they are loved unconditionally but often the truth doesn't penetrate. Questions are a powerful way of dismantling the lies that allow rejection to remain. I am thinking of one person who had insisted repeatedly that they were too much for me to tolerate, too damaged to bother with and that I would soon give up on them and reject them. This went on for several years of counseling.

Finally, after hearing the same lie for the hundredth time I said, "Given all we have been through and all the "reasons" you have given me for rejecting you, I am still here. What makes you think after all this I am going to give up on you and reject you?" I was asking for evidence upon which to continue believing the lie of rejection.

There wasn't any. He had an epiphany – there was no evidence upon which to believe the lie! And I am happy to report that was the end of the lie. The question I asked caused him to examine the evidence, and his own review of our history revealed the lie. He came to the truth himself and so he owned it.

6. Do you understand what I have done for you?

Most of us believe that we communicate effectively, and so we assume that our lesson/message has been received and understood. But what if it hasn't been? The quickest way to find out is to ask. This is what Jesus did the night he washed his disciples' feet. John 13:1-12

Jesus was aware that his death was imminent. This evening was the last opportunity He had to communicate what mattered most to Him, and so He acted out an object lesson in servant leadership. He took the role of the lowliest servant and washed His disciples' feet. So lowly was this act that Peter tried to refuse to allow Jesus to wash his feet.

When He finished washing their feet he returned to His place at the table and asked them a question; **"Do you understand what I have done for you?"** The answer is probably no, because He went on to explain why He did what He did and how He wants them to serve one another. His question was a challenge to them to question whether or not they truly understood His message. It underlines the importance of what Jesus was trying to communicate to them.

Because it is a question, it focused their minds upon the message in a deeper way than if Jesus had just started teaching it. As neuroscience has shown us, when we use questions throughout our training, teaching, counseling, etc., we draw our listeners more deeply into what we are trying to communicate. They become single minded about what we are asking them about. If Jesus chose to lead through questions, perhaps we should as well.

7. Do you love me?

This is the question most of us in a significant relationship want answered. And most of the time we ask for our own benefit, but Jesus was different. When He asked Peter this question it was for Peter's benefit. You probably know the story well. Peter told Jesus that he would lay down his life for Him and Jesus responded by telling him that by morning he would deny Him three times. Perhaps Jesus was warning Peter about the test he was about to face. Warning or not, Peter failed the test - by morning he had denied Jesus three times. Remembering the words of Jesus, Peter's shame must have been excruciating.

The next time Peter sees Jesus it is after Jesus' death and resurrection. Jesus appears to Peter and the other disciples on a beach in the early morning. [John 21:1-19]

After breakfast Jesus asked Peter, **"Do you truly love me more than these?"** By referring to "these", Jesus was referring to the other disciples. Jesus was comparing Peter's love for Him with Peter's love for His peers. In denying Jesus, Peter had valued what others thought of him more than what Jesus thought of him.

By asking Peter this question Jesus is giving Peter the opportunity to examine his heart and correct his failure. Jesus is giving him the chance to restore their relationship. Despite Peter's answer of **"Yes Lord, you know that I love you"**, Jesus repeats the question two more times. Why the repetition? Most commentators agree that because Peter had denied Jesus three times, Jesus was giving him three opportunities to correct his three denials. This is probably the case, but there is another possible reason.

Peter was probably living with overwhelming shame, how could he not, he had denied the most important person in his life. His self-doubt must have been crippling. He needs, not just to tell Jesus how much he loves Him, but to tell himself how

204

much he loves Him. By repeating the question Jesus is giving Peter the opportunity to say "no" to the lies of shame in the deepest way possible. Jesus is giving Peter the way to make a chant of the truth he needs to realize, "YES, I REALLY DO LOVE JESUS!"

Repeating a question is a powerful way of reinforcing the answer. Many truths need to be stated more than once to be believed.

As we have found in our discussion of self-awareness and emotional intelligence, a good leader takes the time to understand the state of mind and emotions of the one he or she leads. To do this is to express love, and love expressed leads to influence gained. More on this in the next chapter, but first...

Some Questions to Consider:

1. Some of Jesus' questions are: 1. What do you want? 2. Do you want to get well? 3. Who do you say I am? 4. What are we going to do about this problem? 5. Where are your accusers? 6. Do you understand what I have done for you? & 7. Do you love me?

2. Notice that all of these questions provoke deeper questions in the one being asked. All of these questions apply to each of us at one time or another. Which one[s] applies to you now?

3. Can you think of a good question to ask someone in whose life you have influence? Might God want to give you one to ask?

4. Ask God to reveal the question He wants to ask you. Take the time to wait for His answer.

Chapter 16: Good Questions from Jesus

The life coaching profession has added a great deal of understanding to the role of using questions to guide individuals [and teams] to good decision making. The role of a good coach is not that of a counselor whose role is to give good advice as to what choice to make. The coach's role is to ask good questions in order to help the coachee to see the issues which bear on the decision, and to help them discover the decision that best fits who they are in the circumstances in which they find themselves. Good questions are vital to this process.

Here are the questions of Jesus categorized by Dale Roach, a coaching expert: [I paraphrase his research and analysis]

1 - Jesus Asks Questions About Doubt

Doubt is a necessary component of faith. It tests the foundation of our faith. It forces us to answer the question, "why do I believe what I believe?"

Here are some examples of Jesus' questions about doubt:

1. Why did you doubt? (Matt. 14:31)

2. Why are you testing me? (Matt. 22:18)

3   If I tell you about earthly things and you will not believe; how will you believe when I tell you of heavenly things? (John 3: 12)

2 - Jesus Asks, "Do You Understand?"

This is an example of using questions to compel the person to search for their own answer to the question, which results in a higher value answer. Here are a variety of Jesus' questions that prompt deeper understanding:

1. **What** profit would there be for one to gain the whole world and forfeit his life and what can one give in exchange for his life? (Matt. 16:26)

2. Salt is good, but **what** if salt becomes flat? (Mark 9:50)

3. **What** king, marching into battle would not first sit down and decide whether with ten thousand troops he can successfully oppose another king marching upon him with twenty thousand troops? (Luke 14:31)

4. If therefore you are not trustworthy with worldly wealth, **who** will trust you with true wealth? (Luke 16:11)

5. **How** is it that you seek praise from one another and not seek the praise that comes from God? (John 5:44)

3 – Jesus Asks, "What Do You Want?" (Matt. 20:32)

As we have already seen, this kind of question makes the person examine their motives and desires at a deep level. By doing so they must take responsibility for answering it.

4 – Jesus Asks Questions From the Bible

Unfortunately, many Christians today would rather call their pastor with a question than take the time to search the Bible for the answer. Many times, Jesus directed His followers to search the Bible for the answers to their questions. Here are two examples:

1. *What did Moses command you? (Mark 10:3)*

2. *What is written in the law? How do you read it? (Luke 10:26)*

5 – Jesus Asks "Why" Questions

When we ask a "why" question we are placing the responsibility on the person to find the answer. We are also provoking them to take the question seriously. We are pushing them to go deeper. Here are some examples of Jesus' "why" questions:

1. Why are you thinking such things in your heart? (Mark 2:8) Why are you anxious about clothes? (Matt. 6:28) (Matt. 8:28)
2. Why do you notice the splinter in your brother's eye yet fail to perceive the wooden beam in your own eye? (Matt. 7:2)
3. Why are you terrified? (Matt. 8:26)
4. Why do you harbor evil thoughts? (Matt. 9:4)
5. Why do you ask me about what is good? (Matt. 19:1)
6. Why does this generation seek a sign? (Mark 8:12)
7. Why were you looking for me? (Luke 2:49)
8. Why do you call me 'Lord, Lord' and not do what I command? (Luke 6:46)

6 – Jesus Asks Faith Questions

As we have already discovered; without questioning our reasons for our faith, our faith becomes weak. I am never surer of my faith than when I have just finished defending it. Here are some of Jesus' "faith" questions:

1. *Where is your faith? (Luke 8:25)*

2. *What are you thinking in your hearts? (Luke 5:22)*

3. *If even the smallest things are beyond your control, why are you anxious about the rest? (Luke 12:26)*

208

4. If I am telling you the truth, why do you not believe me? (John 8:46)

7 – Jesus Asks, "Do You" Questions

These questions prompt deeper thinking, encourage the responsibility for answering their own questions, encourage self-examination, & result in greater self-awareness. Here are a few examples:

1. *Do you realize what I have done for you? (John 13:12)*
2. *Do you also want to leave me? (John 6:67)*
3. *Do you say [what you say about me] on your own or have others been telling you about me? (John 18:34)*
4. *Do you love me? (John 21:16)*
5. *Do you believe I can do this? (Matt. 9:28)*
6. *Do you want to be well? (John 5:6)*

8 – Jesus Asks, "What Are You Discussing With Other People?"

These questions prompt us to consider how the thinking of others is influencing our own conclusions, for better or worse. Here are a few examples:

1. What are you discussing as you walk along? (Luke 24:17)
2. Who do people say the Son of Man is? (Matt. 16:13)
3. But who do you say that I am? (Matt. 16:15)
4. What were you arguing about on the way? (Mark 9:33)

9 – Jesus Asks, "What Are You Trying to Find?"

One of the greatest services we can do for a person is to help them discover what is it they truly want. Everyone is searching for something, and sometimes all they are aware of is the search. Helping them to find their true goal is essential. Here are a few examples of questions that prompt a search:

1. What are you looking for? (John 1:38)
2. What did you go out to the desert to see? (Matt. 11:8)
3. Whom are you looking for? (John 18:4)
4. Do you have eyes and still not see? Ears and not hear? (Mark 8:17-18)"[40]

It should be noted that most of the questions Jesus asked were "open ended", they did not allow for a short answer of either yes or no. The best questions demand serious thought and reflection. They do not just deal with questions of fact, but of emotion, opinion, goals, and dreams. They deal with possibilities and potential, vision and passion, and by so doing they bring us alive to our future and our highest potential.

Recently I had the opportunity to use questions to help guide someone to God's best for his life. Here is his story.

"As my summer vacation was coming to a close, I had a scheduled meeting with our senior leadership team to discuss my Youth Ministry vision for the upcoming school year. Normally this kind of meeting excites me because it's a fresh start and the beginning of a new school season. I also love the aspect of planning and executing a strategy that God has given me. This time was different though. For the first time in 26 years of youth ministry and serving 15 years as the youth pastor at my church I was dreading the meeting with my senior leadership team. I went into the meeting with no vision or new ideas and was feeling unmotivated, discouraged and emotionally exhausted even after a month-long vacation. I felt empty.

After my meeting with Leadership I left feeling even more discouraged and was struggling with the question of how I will be able to get the energy and desire to lead the youth ministry for another year. All the signs seemed to indicate that it was time to step out of youth ministry and step into a new season. But after

26 years and with more than half of my life invested into this ministry I struggled with the thought of "tapping out" and quitting while I had two of my own kids in the youth ministry. I felt like I was at a crossroads and ultimately, I decided that I would just continue on and figure out how to manufacture the motivation and energy to run the youth ministry for another year.

*The next day I made a call to my Associate Pastor Mark to let him know I was going to implement some new ideas for the upcoming year, and I wanted his input. In the middle of our conversation Mark shifted away from the topic and he asked me a very direct and powerful question "Why do you continue to do this?" At first it caught me off guard and I did not respond. He then asked me again "Seriously, why do you do this?" My answer was "This is what I do. I've been doing it for 26 years, I love teenagers, and I have my own kids in the ministry, and I am good at it." That was the beginning to a series of other questions that Mark asked. Each question caused me to think and allowed me to reflect and see a deeper and clearer picture of my heart, and what God was trying to do in my life. When I hung up the phone, I felt like Mark's questions helped me get past my emotions and **allowed me** to come to the conclusion that it was the right time to step out of the ministry I had devoted much of my life to, and into a new season that God was preparing for me. This was a huge step for me but once I made my decision, I felt complete peace with no regrets and knew it was God's will.*

What struck me the most was the process that allowed me to find God's plan for me. Many leaders might have been manipulative or tried to counsel me and tell me what I should do and how I should do it, but Mark never did that. He only asked me questions that allowed me to come to a conclusion that was best for me and where God was trying to lead me to. It was a powerful moment in my life because had Mark not taken the time to ask me those

211

questions, I would have continued down a path away from God's will and that would have robbed me from the full peace and joy that God was trying to give me."

What pleases me most about this account is that I did not try to substitute my conclusion for his. My goal was to simply ask the kind of probing questions that he probably had not asked of himself. My joy is that he remained in charge and responsible for his own choice.

More about asking good questions in the next chapter, but first...

Some Questions to Consider:

1. Jesus asked approximately 175 questions in the 4 gospels. Does this surprise you? Why do you think he used questions so often?

2. Asking good questions takes much longer than simply giving the person the "right" answer. Why is it worth the extra time?

3. Have you ever experienced someone "coaching" you by using good questions?

4. Are you willing to learn how to do it? If your answer is yes, the next chapter is for you.

Chapter 17: How to Ask Good Questions

Not all questions are created equal. Some are helpful, and others are nothing but a distraction. Given the power of asking questions, it behooves us to ask good ones. The value of a question is determined by the goal for which the question is being asked. A leader can be asking a particular question for the personal benefit of the one being led or for the benefit of the leader. For example, let's say the leader is the sales manager of a retailer of consumer household appliances. He is interviewing a salesperson whose numbers are down. He starts the interview with the personal question, "How are your wife and the new baby?"

The sales manager could be asking this question for a number of reasons: 1. Out of genuine personal concern for his employee. 2. He could be asking this question in the hope of discovering an explanation for his salesman's poor performance in order to solve the problem. 3. He could be asking the question out of concern for both. If he is a good leader, it would be because of a concern for both. He has a responsibility to care for his employee as an individual and he has a responsibility to his CEO to sell as many appliances as possible.

The questions to ask will be determined by the goal to be achieved.

Let's change the example somewhat. The salesman has consistently achieved good numbers relative to his fellow salespeople, yet he is growing more and more listless and withdrawn at work. His sales manager has no motive for improving his job performance, so the goal of his questions will be solely for the future well-being of his employee. His concern will be to ask questions that prompt his employee to ask himself where his sense of well-being is coming from.

Questions that cause us to look inside

Questions that deal with dreams, passion, fulfillment, happiness, excitement, and the future are going to be helpful:

- What are you enjoying most about your life right now?
- When do you experience a sense of significance?
- What do you want for your future 10 years from now?
- What stands in the way of fulfilling these desires?
- What would need to happen to remove these obstacles?
- What options do you see available for you?
- What step[s] do you want to take to move forward?

Returning to the example of the salesperson with the declining sales numbers; the questions would be similar but related to the job. For the sake of transparency, the questions should begin with a statement of the manager's concern; "Your sales numbers are down, and I wonder how you are doing. May I ask you some questions about how you are enjoying your job?"

- What are you enjoying most about your job right now?
- When do you experience a sense of significance at work?
- What do you want for your future 10 years from now?
- What stands in the way of fulfilling these desires?
- What would need to happen to remove these obstacles?
- What options do you see available for you?
- What step[s] do you want to take to move forward?

It is interesting to note that the same questions apply for his life goals and his employment goals. The answers he comes up with will often determine whether or not the job is the right fit for who he is as a person. If it is the wrong fit, then his manager has done him a service by helping him to see that. If his job is not the problem, then he now knows he must look elsewhere

214

for the source of his unhappiness. Hopefully he is now on a better track to a better life.

Before going on to another example of asking good questions it is essential to point out that the purpose of listing the 7 possible questions above is not to suggest these questions be asked in a mechanical fashion in the order given. The next question to ask is determined by the last answer given. Good questions arise from the answers given. Questions and answers become a process of exploration for the benefit of discovering a pathway to the goals revealed by the questions.

The next question to ask is determined by the last answer given. Good questions arise from the answers given.

As I have said earlier, it is a sort of detective work in which the person questioned is your partner in his own process of investigative work. There is an art to asking good questions which has nothing to do with having a stable of "good questions" to ask. Fortunately, it is an art that is not hard to learn with practice.

Good questions for the millennial we met earlier

Let's look at how good questions might help our management consultant deal with the millennial I introduced in the first chapter of this book. You may remember, he was employed by a small manufacturing firm in their warehouse loading delivery trucks. He didn't show up for work for several days. He didn't call in sick or give any explanation for why he was absent. Finally, his boss reached him by phone, and they arranged a meeting. At the meeting no resolution was reached, and so the consultant was brought in to deal with the problem. After some discussion it became clear that the employee believed he should be able to set his own hours and days of work per week and do so without consulting with his boss.

The obvious solution is the termination of the employee, which is what ultimately happened, but before that extreme decision was reached, questions could have been asked that may have been valuable to the soon to be unemployed millennial. The first question our consultant might ask is so obvious it might be missed.

"How do you plan to pay for food, shelter, clothing, health care and entertainment?" It seems a simple question with the obvious answer of "by having a job." The fact is, there are a few other alternatives: 1. Live at home with my parents for the rest of my life, 2. Go on welfare, 3. Become a homeless person, 4. Marry a billionaire.

If he answers the question with any of these answers the discussion is over, but if he decides he wants a job then the questioning has just begun. We already know the kind of job he wants; total control over the hours and days worked, with as little responsibility as possible. Here are some good questions to ask:

- What have you done to find a job like that?
- What kind of companies offer a job like that?
- What are the educational requirements for a job like that?
- Who do you know who has a job like that?
- What is your next step to find that job?
- What will your life look like if you don't find it?

Obviously, the purpose of these questions is to begin to ground our soon-to-be unemployed Millennial in the reality of his situation. This is the goal in many such questioning sessions.

Maturity has been defined as the practice of choosing long-term over short-term gains. Short-term gains are often chosen simply because the person has not thought through his future in the light of the benefit of passing up the short-term gain.

216

Good questions often reveal the significant advantages of the long-term gain.

In my own life, most of my important decisions involved choosing between a very attractive short-term gain and a less attractive [but ultimately more advantageous] long-term gain. One of the greatest acts of service that a leader can give is to help those following him to analyze their decisions in the light of their long-term goals. To do so is to acquire increased influence.

Here is another thing to keep in mind when using questions to help direct another person. Don't ask a series of questions you know the answers to. When we do this, it is in effect a cross examination technique. This is what lawyers do to opposing witnesses. It is an obvious effort to lead the witness to a conclusion already chosen by the questioner. Most people recognize leading when it is happening and resent it. It is manipulative and actually creates ill will.

The purpose of asking non-leading questions is to free the person to arrive at their own conclusions. The questions merely help them to avoid illogical or short-sighted conclusions. Most of the value of the conclusion comes from the fact that they have arrived at it for themselves – hence its increased value.

When Jesus asked a sick man what he wanted from Him, He was asking him to examine his desires at their deepest level. At some point in the questioning process I usually ask something like, "If you could control the circumstances of your life, what would you want your life to look like 10 years from now?" Often, we will choose an alternative without measuring its fit with our own deepest desires. Many people have not kept current with their deepest desires and dreams. Simply asking them about them may awaken longings that bring passion, sleeping dreams, and energy to the surface.

Recently I was talking with a cross cultural married couple considering moving out of the country in order to raise their kids in the other culture. The difference between the cultures was significant. Both parents wanted their children to be in touch with the best of both cultures. Both countries offered advantages over the other, in education, job availability, family proximity, etc. It was a very complex decision with many variables.

During the discussion I asked the question, "What do you want your children's lives to look like in 20 years? What educational opportunities do you want for them? What jobs do you want for them? What standard of living? What cultural values do you want them to embrace?" These were questions they had not asked themselves, yet these are vital questions to consider. Once they began to answer these questions, the best conclusion [for them] became apparent. Generally, the deeper the question, the clearer the decision.

The examples of possible questions I have given are very simple questions which most of us would assume the person has already asked themselves. In my experience, most of the time they have not asked themselves these "obvious" questions. The questions they most often overlook are those which deal with their deepest desires and their hopes for the intermediate and later future. For some reason the tyranny of the present "urgent" issues often distracts their attention from the deeper, more important questions. Asking these questions about dreams, deep desires and a hoped-for future often awakens core longings upon which fulfillment rests.

When we ask these deep questions, we are helping the person to become self-aware. Most decision making becomes easier when we know what we really want and, with equal force, what we don't want.

For those readers who lead a team, I refer you to Appendix 2 on page 270 for a very good reference for sample questions you can ask to facilitate growth in your team in these specific areas:

- Conversation Starters
- Confidence Boosters
- Team Builders
- Performance Reviewers

And now I want to leave you with two questions: "What value are good questions if you don't really listen to the answers?" & "How will you know the best question to ask next if you haven't really listened to the last answer?" Loving by listening is the next thing to examine, but first...

A Question to Consider:

Are you willing to try asking questions with a friend who has no crisis to deal with – just for practice? If so, try asking them what concerns they might be dealing with right now. If they give you an answer, try asking them questions about the issue. As they answer your questions try thinking about what question you can ask next that will move them forward in coming up with solutions to their issue. Try to ask questions about what they can do about the problem. This keeps the responsibility for the choice on them. By starting with minor problems or issues you create a safe laboratory in which to experiment and make mistakes. This is where confidence can be built.

Chapter 18: Loving Through Listening

"To answer before listening – that is folly and shame"
Proverbs 18:13

"Everyone should be quick to listen, slow to speak..."
James 1:19

"Being listened to is so close to being loved that most people cannot tell the difference."[41] David Oxberg

"The first duty of love is to listen."[42] Paul Tillich

"To love is to listen, and to listen is to love."
Me -- Mark Cowper-Smith

How I learned to listen

Years ago, our marriage was in trouble. Shelley got sick a few months after our marriage. All of our hopes and dreams for our future were shattered. We both retreated into survival mode – coping became the norm. She became chronically ill.

About 5 years into our marriage I was having my quiet time with God in my back yard. It was another beautiful Southern California morning. I was relaxed and content just to be in the peaceful presence of the Lord. Out of the blue this thought came to my mind, "What is the greatest thing I do for you?" I took this thought to be from God, so I pondered it. I know the correct theological answer is "You died on the cross for my sins" but this is not the answer that came to my mind.

"You really listen to me" is the answer I arrived at.

I think He whispered that answer to me somewhere below my conscious mind because the next thought that came to me was, "You don't listen to your wife." I was deeply convicted of the truth of what He told me. I realized that I had tried to avoid listening to her talk about her pain because it was chronic and there was little, I could do to alleviate it. I said, "What do you want me to do?" The thought [He] said, "You know how you and Shelley go to the community spa every day after work?" I said, "Yes." He said, "I want you to invite her to talk for 30 minutes and I don't want you to interrupt her even once." A deep fear came over me...

Foolishly, I told her what I thought the Lord had said to me. She was THRILLED! She insisted we start that afternoon. That afternoon was the beginning of my lesson on the art of really listening. It was much harder than I thought it would be. It was an exercise in self-control and self-sacrifice. We have been doing it habitually for more than 15 years.

Now it is easy and relaxed, but it is still an exercise in listening.

As a result of this exercise our marriage changed for the better and has been growing better year after year. Seriously! She will be the first to tell you that! My efforts to listen well were the proof of my love for her. To listen is to love, and to love is to listen.

Listening well is more than just not speaking

Of course, there is a catch – listening is much more than simply not speaking. Listening well is an act of focused attention. It requires concentration. It involves putting the other person's world ahead of your own. It is an act of self-sacrifice. Fortunately, it can be learned.

As a writer I can say that finding someone who has said what you want to say, and who has done the research to back up his conclusions, is like finding gold. I found gold when I ran into Erik Barker's blog on skills for listening well.[43]

Here follows a paraphrase of his instructions for good listening:

221

1) Be A Detective

It is a happy coincidence that Barker's first point involves the analogy of being a detective. For years I have used that analogy to describe the process of listening well. The goal is to understand the person you are listening to, to the deepest level possible. Most of the time our listening is nothing more than attempting to be polite while we wait for our turn to speak.

We have already examined the role of asking good questions in order to listen well. The more we can start by asking good questions the easier it is to focus on what we are hearing. After all, we started the process with a question, so it behooves us to listen attentively for the answer.

Start by reminding yourself that you are a detective. As long as the detective is acting out of love, the analogy is perfect.

2) How Little Can You Say?

This instruction is really about self-control. It takes a lot of self-control to resist inserting something about yourself into the conversation. Often something the person says in answer to my question will snag a memory of my own. It is very easy to find yourself saying, "you know something just like that happened to me, let me tell you..." It is at this point that we need to remind ourselves that we are detectives and not witnesses. Try practicing the art of self-control and repeat the mantra "Right now, it's not about me!"

Barker has a short phrase I really like. He says, *"Don't be interesting. Be interested."*

3) Can You Summarize To Their Approval?

At some point it will be time to say something. When that moment comes see if you can summarize what you have heard them say. "Let me see if I have this right. What I hear you saying

222

is..." The goal is to see how accurate you can be in summarizing what they have been saying. If you do it well, you will have communicated much more than that you listened well. You will have communicated that you care about them enough to really listen well. You have made the conversation all about them!

Throughout the narrative you can interject short statements summarizing what they have just said. This sends repeated messages that you are listening. "Wow, the taxi broke down and you had to wait 4 hours in the cold! How did you get home?"

4) Don't Try To Fix Them. Be Socrates.

Socrates taught through the use of questions. His goal was to make people think for themselves to solve their own problems. As we have already found; answers that people arrive at themselves are far more likely to be applied than answers given to them by another. [even when the answers are good ones]

5) Monitor Your Body Language

Communication is not just about the words you choose to use. Communication has an emotional component as well as a physical one. We have already looked at the emotional component in communication. Loving words expressed with angry emotions are nothing but communicational discord. The message is ambiguous at best and usually the emotional content of a message trumps the rational component.

Body language is a legitimate part of communication. Eye contact is extremely important. Barker cites research that suggests that those who listen well make eye contact 70 to 80 percent of the time.

Crossed arms are an obvious sign of impatience or disapproval. Barker cites research that found that "listeners who crossed their arms when they listened retained 38 percent less than listeners who kept their arms at their sides and assumed an open" body posture.

As well, he found research that indicates that touching a person on their elbow is a non-threatening contact that encourages a momentary bond. [Can you believe that someone thought about studying the effect of touching someone on their elbow!?!?]

Avoiding a fatal temptation

Focusing on the skills of good listening brings with it a fatal temptation to believe a half-truth; "by acquiring and practicing the skills of good listening I become a good listener." It is easy to forget that good listening is first and foremost an act of love. When we forget this, we become more of a "professional" than a person. It is the difference between a doctor who sees me as a patient rather than one who sees me as a person. Having had both I can say with certainty that proficiency is essential but having both is what makes a truly great doctor. Listening with your head **and** your heart is what turns listening into love.

Focusing on the skills of good listening brings with it a fatal temptation to believe a half-truth; "by acquiring and practicing the skills of good listening I become a good listener."

Linda Miller and Chad Hall, two Christian coaches have outlined the key factors that turn listening into love.[44]

Here is a summary of their main points: [direct quotes will be in italics]

1. Staying Present and Focused

Let me start with a thought of my own regarding staying present and focused. We live in a world of distraction. Our culture is obsessed with amusement. "Amusement" comes from "a" and "muse." "a" being the opposite of and "muse" being to think. Together they mean "to not think." Essentially, we are a culture seeking not to think. To actually be present for another person just for the purpose of hearing them talk is punishment for most of us. It takes a focus of the will to do it well.

This is why I remind myself every time I am going to try to listen well, that I am a detective searching for clues as to who this person really is. I remind myself that this person is truly interesting, unique, and that coming to really know them will be a rewarding experience. I remind myself that listening well is my gift to them because God loves them. My goal is having a right heart attitude about the act of listening to them. Now back to distractions.

For most of us distractions come so naturally that we don't notice immediately that we are being distracted. Miller and Hall suggest taking the humble approach and admitting to being distracted. Asking the person to repeat their last thought because you were momentarily distracted is both honest and humble. As well, it communicates that you do not want to miss anything they have to say.

Most of us can become aware of the distractions we are most susceptible to. Being forewarned is being forearmed – we know what to look out for. This might mean leaving your smart phone in another room, closing a window to shut out noise, sitting with your back to the window to avoid the view, or consciously deciding to return to your bill paying once the listening session is over.

For me, a habit I have developed for listening to me wife is to pause the TV whenever she enters the room. It sends her the message that I am available to listen to anything she wants to say. In the beginning it was a sacrifice but now it is an act of love that says, "you are more important to me than my entertainment." And it pays great dividends in our relationship. Yes, even during a football game!

Learning to concentrate

Concentration is one of the ways we learn to focus on the person we are listening to. Miller and Hall have a great exercise to develop concentrated listening.

Say each word in your head as another person is speaking:

- *When you are listening to the radio*
- *When you are on the phone*
- *When you are face to face*
- *With your eyes closed [not while driving please!]*
- *With your eyes open*

2. Avoiding Self-Referencing

In my practice of listening, self-referencing is my greatest temptation. A personal experience that relates to their developing story never fails to come to mind. Under other circumstances it might be the perfect thing to interrupt with. We have to keep in mind that the goal here is listening and not teaching or counseling. There is nothing wrong with teaching or counseling as long as it takes place AFTER good listening has taken place.

Here is a good exercise from Miller and Hall to practice self-referencing avoidance.

"Try the following in your everyday conversations: As you practice being present and focused, remove all self-references [comments that include "me" or "I"] from the conversation. Focus only on the person being coached. Write down your perceptions of the difference it makes."

226

Here are their tips for great listening:

- *Maintain eye contact when face to face*
- *Reduce visual distractions, especially when on the phone.*
- *Put phones and e-mails on silent mode so they don't intrude on the conversation*
- *Determine ways to reduce mental distractions*
- *Allow for silences instead of immediately jumping in with something*
- *Be aware when you are interrupting... stop it!*
- *Relax and pay attention to all that is being said.*
- *If necessary, take notes to stay focused and to remember details*
- *Take two to three minutes of quiet time before you are called on to be an active and present listener. Take a few deep breaths, say a prayer, and determine what will help you to be ready to listen.*

3. Paying Attention to Your Own Thoughts While Listening

It is possible to be a present and focused listener and, at the same time, pay attention to your own thoughts in three important areas: [I am paraphrasing again]

- Precise Questions that need to be asked. [We have discussed this type of question in a previous chapter.]
- Reminders to suspend judgement. It is easy to see bad decisions, attitudes and sins while listening to someone discuss his problems, and so it is tempting to jump in to teach a "life lesson." This rarely works out well. We can trust God to convict of failure and sin when He wants to. Our job is to listen well.
- Commentary [and insight] on what is being said. This is the awareness of themes and important issues arising from the person we are listening to, e.g. fear, failure,

hope, trust, etc. This internal commentary often helps us to choose the next precise question to ask.

"Finally, along with listening to self and listening to the person being coached, the Christian coach also listens for the still, small voice or the "gentle whisper" of the Lord. [1 Kings 19:12] The wise coach can enter each coaching conversation prayerfully and expectantly, prepared to hear and respond to holy "nudges" from the Holy Spirit."

At this point in our discussion of focused listening I anticipate a question; "Am I supposed to approach every conversation I have with everyone as a coaching conversation?" The answer is "no" but, given our human tendency to listen poorly, the more we practice these coaching listening techniques the better our "normal" listening will become. Our influence will grow as our listening improves because, "to listen is to love."

Because we have spent so much time discussing the technique of good listening it is easy to forget that the point of listening is love. Here are words of wisdom from someone who paid the ultimate price in learning the truth of what he says.

Dietrich Bonhoeffer was an up-and-coming theologian in Germany during the rise of Hitler. Bonhoeffer had the opportunity to leave Germany and avoid falling prey to the wrath of the Third Reich. He chose to stay and, prior to his imprisonment and martyrdom at the hands of the Nazis, he led an underground seminary community. In his book, Life Together[42], he describes several essential ministries that a genuine Christian community must have. The first is listening. In his own words:

> *"The first service that one owes to others in the fellowship consists in listening to them. Just as love to God begins with listening to His Word, so the beginning of love for the brethren is learning to listen to them. It is God's love for us*

that he not only gives us His Word but also lends us His ear... Christians, especially ministers, so often think they must always contribute something when they are in the company of others, that this is the one service they have to render. They forget that listening can be a greater service than speaking."[45]

Listening well is an act of self-sacrifice. It requires focus and concentration. It is difficult, so why bother? Three reasons come to mind; first, it is one of the best ways to say no to your pride and self-focus, second, it is an act of love which will always be appreciated, & third, it leads to greater influence.

On to more ways we can lead through love, but first...

Some Questions to Consider:

1. What can you do to remain present and focused while listening?

2. What can you do to avoid self-referencing while listening?

3. What can you do to pay attention to your own thoughts while listening that pertain to; a) Precise questions that need to be asked, b) Reminders to suspend judgements of the person, & c) Your own internal commentary on what is being said, for the purpose of choosing the next precise question to ask.

   We will often make internal commentary to ourselves about a developing theme in what we are hearing. For example, "I noticed he mention fear four times since he started talking... time to ask a question about fear."

Chapter 19: Putting People Ahead of the Vision

My friend has an expression he uses when discussing success as defined by some church leaders. He calls it the "Noses and Nickels" standard of success. How many people are in our church and how much money do they bring in? It sounds like a business, doesn't it? And therein lies the problem. A business exists to sell a product or service to customers or clients. Traditionally, those who are employees of the business are there for that reason alone, to serve the customers. Can the same be said of a family or a church?

The business of a family is to maximize the well-being of each member - it serves its members. A church is a faith family. It exists to maximize the spiritual growth of each member, at least it should. The spiritual growth of each member includes an outward vision, reaching the lost, but it is not defined only by that goal.

"Noses and Nickels" doesn't equate to success if the church's members are seen as nothing but resources to be deployed to further the leader's vision of success. A good church can say with integrity "Come here and you will be loved" rather than, "Come here and you will be used." All this to say, in God's Kingdom the people are the vision.

> **A good church can say with integrity *"Come here and you will be loved"* rather than, *"Come here and you will***

In this chapter and the next we will discuss 4 ways that a family, church or business can make people the vision. They are 1. Being an approachable and available leader, 2. Building community, 3. Identifying and facilitating people's callings, & 4. Celebrating your people's success.

Being an approachable and available leader

In the survey I have previously discussed, the respondents frequently cited being available as one of the characteristics of those to whom they granted influence.

Nothing says "you matter to me" as much as putting aside a pressing matter to make time for someone who needs someone to talk to. It is an act of sacrifice and so it is experienced as an act of love.

> **Nothing says "you matter to me" as much as putting aside a pressing matter to make time for someone who needs someone to talk to.**

Of course, a senior leader cannot have time for everyone in the organization they lead, but he can make time for those who report directly to him. The "open door" may have to be scheduled in advance as blocks of time during which those you lead know the door is open and the welcome mat is in front of it.

I am mentally imagining a probable response to what I have just written; *"What about those people who abuse my time and simply want constant attention, even when they have no real need for it?"* The truth is, every one of us in leadership has had people like this in our lives. If you haven't... just wait... they will come. The problem is that we often base our solution on solving the problem of the exception, rather than basing it on the rule. It is too easy to over-react to the rare problem person and end up neglecting those who have a genuine need to connect with their leader.

As well, slowing down to pastor the "clingy" one takes time. It may seem like a waste of valuable time, but just taking the time to explain why you cannot be available all the time, is an example of being approachable.

Here is another quote from Dietrich Bonhoeffer in his book, "Life Together." It deals with the second essential ministry for genuine Christian community. The first is listening [which we have discussed in the last chapter] and the second is what he calls "the ministry of helpfulness." In his own words:

> "The second service that one should perform for another in a Christian community is that of active helpfulness. This means, initially, simple assistance in trifling, external matters...One who worries about the loss of time that such petty, outward acts of helpfulness entail is usually taking the importance of his own career too solemnly.

> We must be ready to allow ourselves to be interrupted by God. God will be constantly crossing our paths and canceling our plans by sending us people with claims and petitions. We may pass them by, preoccupied with our more important tasks, as the priest passed by the man who had fallen among thieves... It is a strange fact that Christians and even ministers frequently consider their work so important and urgent that they will allow nothing to disturb them... They think they are doing God a service in this...But it is part of the discipline of humility that we must not spare our hand where it can perform a service and that we do not assume that our schedule is our own to manage but allow it to be arranged by God." [46]

I read these words early in my leadership career and they went straight to my heart. I recognized myself in them. I have never forgotten them. It wounds me when I see leaders that consider themselves too busy to spend time with their team. A while ago we had a new family come to our church. He had been employed as a youth pastor at a mega church for more than 5 years.

Shortly after their arrival at our church, our senior pastor took them out for lunch. They were shocked and they told him why. It turns out that not once in 5 years of serving in his previous church, did he ever have a conversation with his senior pastor!

James' story

James joined the staff of a large mega church, having come from a successful career as a businessman. It was his first paid ministry position. His senior pastor was a great teacher and James looked forward to learning from such a wise and successful Christian leader. Here is his story in his own words.

I was hired as a pastoral staff member at a large church. It was my first full-time ministry position. I had worked as a volunteer for many years but knew I was called to full-time ministry. When I got the phone call, I was beside myself with joy.

But as the days, weeks, and months went by I wondered why the senior pastor never spent personal time with me. I asked others why and they simply said that he didn't build relationships with anybody. I had a difficult time with this for two reasons: First, it was unbiblical. I saw Jesus spending a tremendous amount of time with his disciples. And secondly, my definition of Christianity is relationship – with God and others - so it was a huge disconnect for me to be assigned the task of building relationships with those who were under my care, and yet the person whose care I was under wasn't developing a relationship with me. And furthermore, besides receiving revelation from his preaching, there are certain things that can only come through a personal relationship, like Paul and Timothy, Elijah and Elisha, and Moses and Joshua experienced. I felt I was getting robbed.

So, I got up the courage to go speak to him about it. I went into his office and said, "Pastor, I was wondering why you don't develop relationships with people on your team." His response stunned me. Don't get me wrong, I love this man. He has done a tremendous amount of good and has led hundreds, if not thousands, of people to Christ. But in the area of personal relationships, he came from a generation who were actually taught not to get close to those on your staff. So, after I asked that question, he just looked at me with his very gentle, kind eyes and said, "I don't need it." That is exactly what he said that he didn't need it. We just stood there and stared at each other, awkwardly. I finally replied, "But we do." Then it got even more awkward. We just stared at each other some more, then he just gave a nervous chuckled and said something like, "We'll see" and walked back to his desk. That was the end of that! And the situation never changed.

This incident provides a good transition into our next subject.

Building community

The Apostle Paul uses two analogies to describe the Church of Jesus Christ: as a family and as an army.

A Family: **"... let us do good to all people, especially to those who belong to the family of believers."** Galatians 6:10

An Army: **"Endure hardship with us like a good soldier of Christ Jesus. No one serving as a soldier gets involved in civilian affairs – he wants to please his commanding officer."** 2 Timothy 2:3-4

Church as an army vs. church as a family

This is interesting because they are very different. My friend Dr. Ken Blue illustrates the differences with a series of questions.

	ARMY	FAMILY
1. Focus?	the mission	relationships
2. Purpose?	to fight	to love
3. Discipline?	total obedience for victory	minimum necessary for fairness
4. Favorite companion?	the meanest warrior	the nicest one
5. Most important person?	the General	the one hurting now
6. Pastor's role?	leader	father or mother

At the same time, the church is to be both a family and an army. Sounds like multiple personality disorder doesn't it? Yet, these two roles happen to coincide with the two deepest desires of most Christians. Most of us yearn for two things:

1. To be accepted for who I am right now with all my faults. We all yearn to be loved and valued without having to perform to earn it. We just want to belong. The church as a family was designed to give us this. It is called grace.
2. Not to be left as I am right now, with all my faults. We want to grow to become all God designed us to be. Our prayer is, "Accept me as I am, but please don't leave me this way!" The church as an army was designed to do this for us. It is called holiness.

In any given moment we want one more than the other, but deep down inside we know we want both. We want both because we need both – by God's design.

Our default preference

What is interesting is that most of us gravitate to one or the other, again by God's design. We have a default position. Because of our genetics and past experiences or trauma, most of us are drawn to either family or army. And this is true for our leaders as well. When I teach this lesson in a conference most people have no trouble determining their bias. It is important to know that there is no right answer. What is important is to know your present need and your default preference.

This is especially important for leaders because the church will conform to the default preference of the leadership. This would be fine if God wanted every church to be either a "family" church or an "army" church, but He wants each church to be a healthy balance of the two. To be balanced, the leadership needs to recognize its default preference and to take steps to strive for a healthy balance. Naturally, this creates tension within the individual leader and within the leadership as a team. Let's look at the role of our spiritual leaders under both Army and Family.

ARMY	FAMILY
training for the mission	comfort for the people
battle strategy	healing broken people
issuing commands	giving counsel & advice
ensuring obedience/discipline	ensuring interdependence
a spiritual "general"	a spiritual father or mother

These preferences apply to all relationships

A good balance between *army* and *family* is a goal not just for pastors, but for all of us. We are all in leadership positions or positions of influence within the relationships that make up our lives. Fathers, mothers, sisters, brothers, co-workers, friends, employers and employees all lead by way of positions of authority or positions of influence, from time to time and situation to situation.

We all have our natural default preference regarding "family" or "army." It would be easiest for us to simply say, "I am an army guy, so just suck it up and live with it!" As tempting as this is, the godly question to ask is not "which is natural and easiest for me?" but rather, "What does the person in front of me right now need – a spiritual general or a spiritual father, mother or friend?"

The same question applies in the life of a church. Sometimes the church needs to be challenged and other times it needs to be comforted. Only the Holy Spirit can overcome our default preference and guide us into which is best for the person or the church in this season. There is no easy religious formula to follow except to recognize our own God-designed default preference, and to allow God and **others** to draw us to the balance that is best for those we love and serve.

Notice that I said "others" as well as God. Being married and being a part of a leadership team - both confront us with others who do not share our default preference. In fact, often we are teamed up with someone who is our opposite. This is by God's design and is for the good of the marriage, the church, or both. **We need those who disagree with us as much as those who agree with us – actually we need them even more.**

So, where does this leave each of us? How can we apply this to our lives? What do we need to keep in mind?

1. God designed the church to live in the tension between being a family and being an army. This means that the tension is good for us and we should stop trying to avoid it!
2. God's design and my past experience/trauma result in a bias in me toward one or the other. My default preference is neither good nor bad, but if it came about through trauma, the God-designed balance for me cannot come about until I

receive healing for the trauma. Don't refuse to face the trauma.

3. In order to live well in the tension between the two, I need those around me who do not share my default preference. They are a gift from God for me. Welcome your critics, they might be speaking for God.

4. I am a person of influence. I am a leader in certain relationships within my life. **As a person of influence or a leader, I have a God ordained responsibility to do my best to be what the person before me right now needs, either for their comfort or for their growth.** It is not OK for me to defer to my default preference without asking the Holy Spirit to guide me to be what is most needed in the moment. All we have discussed about emotional intelligence, asking good questions and listening well come into play at the moment of determining what is best for the person I am influencing.

5. I have no right to judge my leaders because they do not share my default preference, but I am free to speak to them from it.

6. As a leader, I have no right to judge those I lead because they do not share my default preference, but I am free to speak to them from it.

7. The question in every case is what does this person/church need most? What is most helpful? What is most loving?

8. A healthy family, church or leadership team is one which is balanced, with both family and army voices being heard.

A healthy family, church or leadership team is one which is balanced, with both family and army voices being heard.

It should be clear what my bias is, but in the interest of being transparent, my bias is toward seeing the church as a family first.

It is hard not to reach this conclusion when considering the nature of God. He is three persons in one. I like to say that God doesn't merely value relationships, He is a relationship. He is love in love with love. What I understand this to mean is that He is best revealed through our relationships in the body of Christ – the church. John puts it very clearly when he says,

"No one has ever seen God; but if we love one another, God lives in us and his love is made complete in us." 1 John 4:12

The quintessential nature of God is revealed when we love one another. This truth compels us to value "family" very highly. I believe that when we strive for a balance between family and army, we will end up with a family that can fight like an army and an army that can love like a family – the best of both.

Building a Christian community means being a leader who is continually monitoring the relationships in his team. He is looking for where the relationships are being challenged. He is watching for miscommunication, misunderstandings, unforgiveness, lack of transparency and vulnerability, judgementalism, pride, disrespect, etc. He is not afraid to bring these things into the light, even when he is the one who is at fault. In this regard he is acting as a good father protecting the family's relationships.

Building a Christian community means taking time away from the task to spend it on purely relational time together. We need to know each other for more than what we bring to the work we do. This means having fun together. Our staff team still talks about the best staff retreat we ever had.

Our leader was prepared to delve into deep spiritual issues with our team. On the way to the retreat center the Lord spoke to him and told him to throw away his agenda and just have fun with us. We ended up playing charades until after midnight – the laughter never ceased! We end up laughing all over again when we describe that retreat to new staff members. These shared memories of non-work times are precious. They remind us that we are more than what we do, and that the Christian life is much more than work. Every month we spend one staff meeting having dinner together talking about our lives, and the CHURCH PAYS!

Another story from James

Before we leave the family/army dichotomy James has one more story that illustrates a severe "army" imbalance. In his own words.

> On another occasion, immediately after I was hired, I wanted to ask to leave early on Fridays so I could go home and prepare for a Friday night service that I led each week at the church. I went to my pastor's office and saw that he was in, so I knocked. He graciously welcomed me in and listened to my request. I felt we found a place of common ground and developed a bit of a bond as we talked about preaching and the privilege of feeding God's sheep. It was really a wonderful experience. I felt like we truly understood each other.
>
> Well, that next Monday the pastor's wife called me into her office. As I entered, I saw two long-time staff members sitting in chairs, looking at the ground. I thought someone had died. The look on her face was stern and serious. She then began chastising me for going around her and directly to the pastor. I thought it was a joke at first, but as I looked at the other guys in the room to see if they were chuckling, they were still just staring at their shoes. It took me a moment to realize that she was serious! You see, she was the personnel manager, and EVERYTHING had to be run through her. Now I wasn't new to managing teams – I had been a general manager of multiple stores

240

and understood systems and protocol, but all I had done was walk downstairs from my office in the church, saw the pastor in his office (no one else was there as it was a Friday afternoon) and asked for this small concession. This was my first experience of church as a business and how seriously a person can take their title and protect their turf.

The next thing I did was obviously a cardinal sin – I asked for the reasoning behind a pastoral team member not having direct access to the lead pastor. You would have thought I insulted the Trinity! She launched into a speech that was paramount to a parent scolding her two-year old. When she was done (and as the other two were still starring at their shoes) I said, "I just want to go back to work." I meant back to my desk upstairs, but she replied, "Yes, I think it would be best if you went back into the business world." She was actually going to fire me!!! Wow. Unbelievable. Well, I knew God had prepared more for that position and that it was His will that I work there so I clarified my statement, apologized for my misstep with protocol, and said I would never do it again. (I was beginning to feel like the other two in the room!) She accepted my apology and ended the meeting. This was my first experience of church as a business and how seriously a person can take their title to protect their turf.

Here's a good motto – keep people first. More on how we do this, but first...

Some Questions to Consider:

1. Have you ever had a leader who makes time for you even when it is difficult for him or her? If so, what affect did his or her availability have on you?

2. Bonhoeffer says that when we are interrupted by people, we are often being interrupted by God. Does this change your view of being interrupted? If so, how?

3. Do you gravitate to seeing the church as principally a family or an army? Was your father a family type leader or an army type leader? Or a balance of the two?

4. Can a church be both a family and an army? If yes, how can it do that?

5. Does your church need to move more in an army or family direction?

6. What is the role of listening well to achieve a balance between family and army?

Chapter 20: Celebrating Callings & Successes

One of the ways a leader can keep people first is by being committed to helping people to fulfill their ministry callings. God births a calling into every new believer. It is part of their spiritual DNA. Significance and fulfillment come when we discover what we were designed for and do it. Each of us has our own personal "vision" - that passion that fuels our efforts. Back in the day they called it our "vocation."

To a visionary leader the last paragraph might sound threatening. After all, doesn't the leader establish the vision of the church? Isn't it true that there is only room for one vision in the church? The truth is there is only one vision for the church collectively, but the church is filled with people waiting for their personal visions to be revealed and fulfilled. Being a win/win God, He has designed the collective vision of the church to be advanced through the fulfillment of each individual's vision or calling.

Identifying dreams and callings

> **The task of a visionary leader is to help each church member to discover their calling and to use it to advance the collective vision of the church.**

The task of a visionary leader is to help each church member to discover their calling and to use it to advance the collective vision of the church. God does not give visions or callings to function other than for,the benefit of the local church. Ultimately, successful parachurch visions aid the edification of the local church. This happens through evangelism where converts brought to faith in a parachurch ministry find local churches to disciple them throughout their lives. It also happens where parachurch or trans-local ministries aid the church in its task of discipleship, e.g. Focus on the Family.

It is the challenge of a "people first" visionary leader to find ways for each member to apply his own vision and passion to serve the vision of the local church.

I have been using the term "visionary leader" which subtly suggests there is another kind of leader, a visionless leader. A leader without a vision is not a leader, he is a maintenance man. To be a leader is to have a vision, but the vision may be "vision first" or "people first." The difference is in how the vision is advanced. A visionary leader can either push or pull people toward the vision.

Push or pull?

Pushing the people toward the vision puts the vision first. Positional leadership is the first choice of those who push. It either uses some sort of force or some sort of manipulation to motivate the people to serve the vision. It is ultimately short sighted because it uses external motivation to keep the workers on task.

As we have found, external motivation requires continual supervision to enforce. It also leads to burn out. In a volunteer organization like a church, it often leads to a failure of the vision. The irony is that the vision is usually not at fault. A godly vision being pursued in an ungodly way will fail. The means, as well as the ends, must be godly.

Pulling the people toward the vision puts the people first because it appeals to internal motivation. Pulling people toward the vision can only be done through influence. So how does this "pulling" work?

The short answer is through all the factors we have discussed which increase a leader's influence.

Picture this

I have a mental image that might clarify the process. Our first image is of a leader standing behind a person and literally pushing them forward toward the fulfilment of the vision. In this image the people are ambivalent about the vision.

Our second image requires a little more imagination. Imagine the leader has the ability to reach inside the follower and touch his soul. When the leader touches his soul, or more commonly his "heart", he awakens his deepest longings for significance and purpose. The leader also speaks with so much passion about the beauty of the vision that the follower finds his passion being enflamed. He "sees" himself as contributing something extremely valuable to the vision. He sees himself giving himself to something bigger than himself - bigger than anything he could ever do on his own. He is drawn to the vision and he "catches" it.

Where does he fit?

At this point the issue becomes, how can he best serve the vision? A positional leader would answer this question by examining the vision to determine what needs are as yet un-met. He would then assign the enthusiastic follower to the job that needed to be done. This is the "warm body" approach – any warm body will do. This is a vision first, people second approach.

An influential leader would approach the issue in the reverse order. He would start by examining the follower to discover who he really is. He would do this with good questions, good listening, good emotional intelligence, being available to the follower and with the best interests of the follower in mind.

Once he truly knows who the follower is, he will try to place him in the position that will best fulfill the follower first... and then the vision. He will always maintain the goal to never set anyone up for failure. If the vision will have to wait for the right person to appear, so be it.

A method for facilitating dreams and callings

Rick Warren of Saddle Back Church has developed a program to make it easy to ask the right questions. The program is called S.H.A.P.E. The acronym stands for; Spiritual Gifts, Heart [or Passion], Natural Abilities, Personality, & Life Experience. The goal of the program is to place a volunteer or employee in the ministry or job that is most suited to the person they are.

The rationale is as follows.

1. In order for a person to flourish in a ministry role they need to be using their spiritual gifts. These are those Holy Spirit given gifts, and empowered abilities, that will bring the love of God to those they serve.

2. In order for people to have staying power in a ministry role they should be serving in the area of their passion. People who are serving in the area of their passions do not need to be constantly encouraged to give their best – they want to give their best! If anything, the leader's task in leading them will be to make sure they don't overwork! A person's passion is easy to discover with a simple question; "If you had unlimited time, energy, money and talent what would you do?"

3. God never wastes anything He has built into us. Our natural talents are a resource that should be used in pursuit of our vision. We see this illustrated in the lives of many Christian athletes. Their natural talent and hard work have given them a platform of credibility with millions of people. It should be used

in pursuit of their passion and in a way that utilizes their spiritual gifts.

5. Personalities vary according to God's design. Don't ask an introvert to speak in front of thousands of people and don't tell an extrovert not to.

Don't ask an introvert to speak in front of thousands of people and don't tell an extrovert not to.

6. God never wastes our life experiences, even the bad ones. What we have experienced shapes us into who we are at present. [for good or bad] I have noticed that often the best ministry to the broken is done by those who have experienced deep brokenness. Someone who has been where you are now has a credibility that no one else has. We are drawn to those who understand us, because they have been where we are. For us, they are people of influence.

This is a very abbreviated explanation of what is a very helpful resource. I highly recommend it to you. What it is doing is using a questionnaire to ask good questions. Used with love and concern for the best interests of those seeking to be spiritually employed, it makes the process of finding the right fit for each follower much easier.

I wonder if some of you are asking the question, "What about those people who have a vision for ministry outside the local church?" In my experience it is hard to imagine an external vision that does not in some way benefit the local church. Serving the lost is a means of evangelism. So are foreign missions. It may happen that we find someone whose S.H.A.P.E. profile does not work for our church. The solution is the help them find the church where it does fit. This is simply putting the person ahead of our vision. We get points for this in heaven.

Before we leave this subject there is one more advantage to seeking to fulfill people's ministry callings. It assumes that the best visions have not been discovered yet. The more we seek to help those we lead to discover and pursue their ministry dreams and callings, the more ministry we birth into our Christian community. The best is yet to come...

Celebrate Your People's Success

"After a long time the master of those servants returned and settled accounts with them. The man who had received five bags of gold brought the other five. 'Master,' he said, 'you entrusted me with five bags of gold. See, I have gained five more.' His master replied, 'Well done, good and faithful servant! You have been faithful with a few things; I will put you in charge of many things. Come and share your master's happiness!'" Matthew 25:19-21

This is part of a story Jesus told dealing with how God responds to His faithful servants. The servant has used his gifts and talents to his best abilities and the Master acknowledges that fact and ends by saying "Come and share your master's happiness." Clearly God intends to celebrate our faithful obedience. And we should do likewise with those who serve faithfully with us.

"One of the most important things I've learned from being a football coach and a pastor is that you cannot celebrate your team's victories often enough."[47] Tom Mullins, author of The Leadership Game

Mullin summarizes five benefits to celebrating your followers' successes. I will paraphrase his points.

1. Celebration demonstrates that you value your team

To celebrate another's success is to love them. It imparts value to the person. It is inherently positive and hence faith building for everyone on the team. It says to everyone on the team, "we could be celebrating your success next!"

2. Celebration reinforces core organizational values

Whatever the leader is celebrating in the person is reinforced to the whole team. It is important to note that the leader must be living the values he is celebrating. Leading by example is a key source of influence and without it celebrating values that are not being lived by the leader rings hollow for everyone.

3. Celebration builds team morale

Sharing the joy of a victory allows everyone to experience joy. This shared joy is a powerful team building experience. It is hard to find a person who doesn't enjoy a celebration. Mullen makes a point that emphasizes one of our powerful sources of influence.

"I have found that one of the most motivating things I can do to serve and celebrate my team members is to take time to learn how each person is uniquely motivated. It is the leader's responsibility to learn what each team member values and how that person prefers to celebrate." [48] Tom Mullins

His point illustrates the importance of emotional intelligence. Being sensitive to how the person responds to praise and how it is given amounts to high EQ. Taking the time to ask the right questions shows love for the follower and leads to an increase in the leader's influence. This can be done one on one, but it can also be a team building discussion.

4. Celebration increases retention and productivity

Mullin mentions a statistic that we have already examined. According to the US Department of Labor, 46 percent of those who leave their jobs do so because they feel underappreciated. This is entirely the fault of their leader. Celebrating team members' successes is a powerful antidote to feeling underappreciated. As we have already seen, so is listening to them.

He also notes that happy workers are productive workers. In Mullin's words, *"what gets celebrated gets done!"*

5. Celebration is a great recruiting tool

In Mullins words, *"Celebration also serves as a great recruiting tool for your organization. I've found that when a recruit witnesses the ways we celebrate wins together as a team, they are eager to be a part of what's happening here. Celebration is attractive partly due to its rarity in many organizations."* [49]

Some Questions to Consider:

1. What is the difference between a leader who "pushes" people toward his vision and one who "pulls" them toward it? Have you experienced both types? If yes, which worked best for you?

2. Are you aware of your personal S.H.A.P.E. profile? If not, how do you think knowing it would change your approach to ministry?

3. Have you ever had a leader who celebrated your successes? What affect did it have on you?

Chapter 21: What if I Make a Mistake?

My wife has worked with families in crisis since 1984. She provided a home to 24 high risk foster teenagers [2 at a time]. As well, she worked for private and public agencies helping families. She asked if she could submit a chapter on repair. She feels if kids don't learn from their parents how to repair relationships, they won't know how to repair any of their relationships. This will impact their future friendships, education, and employment.

If young people learn how to repair relationships, they can build a healthy workplace instead of one filled with tension. When they become parents, instead of bringing tension home to their families, they can start a new cycle. The family unit gets stronger instead of weaker. Our culture needs strong families.

In order to break out of dysfunctional cycles, we need to start with ourselves. Understanding that we are the only person that we can control is crucial. It starts with each of us making significant changes in our thinking. Fortunately, we can learn to do this.

And now, wisdom from Shelley.

It has been a privilege to see hundreds of people come to self-awareness, take responsibility, and repair relationships. That includes me! Learning to repair my own relationships has been a continual "work in progress."

But it is possible!

There are skills we can learn. And these skills set us up to increase our joy and influence in all our relationships. There is a learning curve though. So, stick with us here. Let's work through it.

By this point in the book, you may have recognized mistakes you've made in relationships. If you haven't, you may need to go back to review the section on self-awareness? Just saying...

Mark says it well in Chapter 10:

Relationships thrive on honesty and die because of falsehood. I have done countless hours of marriage counseling and know, from painful experience, that once a spouse has been lied to, the issue is the restoration of trust. Restoration of trust does not come easily, and why should it? "If he's lied to me once how do I know he won't lie to me again?" Broken promises lead to broken relationships.

Repair is possible.

The truth is we all make mistakes. Self-awareness of our mistakes is crucial. Repair begins when we become aware of our mistakes and take ownership.

Ownership means the willingness to face the uncomfortable things in life. It is an *"assertive"* as opposed to a *"passive"* response. It doesn't accept the belief that "time heals all wounds."

Sometimes, time does provide the space for perspective and correction. Most of the time however, we need intentional skills, and the tools, to make changes within ourselves to repair relationships.

If we do not learn these tools and develop these skills, we may find ourselves subconsciously avoiding relationships because they seem too unpleasant. There is a better way. Repair is possible.

Common thoughts about repair

Here are three common objections you might have heard or find yourself thinking.

Objection #1 - I'm not the type of person to look back

"Life is about moving forward and making progress. There is too much to be accomplished to sit around wondering why things happened. It is best to just keep moving and do our best. Afterall, nobody is perfect!"

Some personalities gravitate to a strong focus on the future and do not see the purpose in reflection and evaluation. They value emotional "toughness" and are critical of those who want to review and repair situations. For every one of these there is someone thinking

"I need more time to process what just happened... Why is everyone in such a rush to move on? What about the people that are still hurting? What do we need to learn about here? Is something wrong with me that I still have some questions and thoughts about what just happened?"

Some personalities take a longer time to process events and often feel rushed and critical of those who want to move on. The trouble here is; there is no easy compromise between a fast and slow processor. One or more of the parties are going to feel thwarted and frustrated.

Objection #2 - It doesn't work

She had already said she was sorry, so she didn't understand his attitude towards her. "I took the high road and humbled myself! I am not going to do any more than that. People have told me I did more than I needed to, so I am done with this relationship. He is too sensitive."

As I spoke with the other party, he shared his confusion as well.

"She came to me to talk and explain all the reasons she made such a rash decision that affected my role in the company. She felt I moved too slowly on things, so she had to do something for the good of the company. She said sorry if it hurt me but that it had to be done. I am just not sure what she was saying. Was she sorry or was she using the opportunity to teach me about my weakness of going too slow? I have lost my trust in her and feel I need to keep my distance."

Conversations like these happen far more than we realize. Some people find it easier to avoid a person than to clean up and repair mistakes.

Objection #3 - It's too uncomfortable

"I know I made a mistake, and I did my best to make things better right away. I didn't want to focus on the negative too long so I just did my best, that is all anyone can ask. I don't want to think about it anymore."

This type of thinker shows a willingness to attempt to repair his mistakes but stops when it becomes too uncomfortable. He may do a shallow exploration of his actions and offer a quick apology but neglect to stick with the process long enough for the root issues to be explored.

What does work?

You may have heard of Steven Covey's popular book, "7 Habits of Highly Effective People." His son Steven M. Covey worked with his dad and then did consulting for 100's of companies that all had one thing in common - their undealt with mistakes cost them big time! They had lost the trust of their employees, board members and customers. And trust is everything.

I remember when we merged our company, Covey Substantive with Franklin Quest. We'd been arched competitors. We formed Franklin Covey from that merger. We'd been arched competitors

254

before and we were both two good companies, good people, with good values, coming together. But people didn't trust each other because of the fact that we had been competitive and coming at it from different angles and so while I had seen the advantages of high trust, I suddenly also saw the high cost of low trust.

Then we made conscious, deliberate efforts to get to build and rebuild the trust and to get good at this and I saw that we could do that. We could actually make progress. It didn't have to be what it was. We could move to the level of trust, consciously and deliberately.[1]

How do we build trust?

We see in the example above, trust was not established as a priority, and as a result was diminishing. Trust is never stagnant. It is either growing or shrinking. It can be like a tank with a hole in it that leaks at high speed. Repairing the hole in the tank may require not only an apology, but significant filling as well.

The research and literature for emotional intelligence has brought us further in understanding ourselves and others. Often, however, it hasn't provided us with many of the skills necessary to repair damaged relationships. And the sophisticated courses that do cover repair skills are often complicated and difficult to remember. If it is not easy, we often give up before the skills become part of our lives.

The rest of this chapter will describe four clear steps to process situations and make good decisions. We will give an example of how they work and present four additional skills for strengthening all relationships.

---

[1] Biznews Digest: Stephen Covey: Why trust is the new must – tips on how to start building it written August 23, 2016, by Alec Hogg

FOUR STEPS FOR PROCESSING SITUATIONS:

1. Connect

2. Clarify

3. Consider

4. Choose

Imagine putting the situation in the center of a room and walking around it. We will examine the situation from various angles with three simple questions. This will increase our awareness and perspective. The process will conclude with the forth step of making an informed choice. The process is easy to remember so you can repeat it often. The more we practice, the quicker we become. I can complete these four steps in under 3 minutes. Using this process will save so much time in the long run.

Pause for a moment and think of the time you might save when you make informed choices instead of subconscious reactions.

Example:

Maria knew she had a strained relationship with her daughter but did not know what she could do about it. She was trying really hard to be a better mom and could go days without an argument. But she felt like she took 3 steps forward and 2 steps back as the inevitable argument would erupt and they would both end up in a bad mood. Sometimes she felt it was pointless to keep trying. It felt like living her youth all over again. It was just too painful.

Step #1 - Connect

Maria's situation repeats itself in all of her relationships. She gets to point of discouragement and pulls away from her friends, coworkers, boss, and even those she supervises. She has uncomfortable emotions and doesn't know what to do with them. So her choice is to disconnect from others. In reality what is also happening is she is disconnecting from herself. She puts a wall around her negative feelings and keeps busy to avoid any of the unpleasant feelings and thoughts.

So the first step is to slow down and ask three questions:

1. How can I connect with myself instead of trying to ignore what is going on inside of me?

2. How can I connect with God?

3. How will this help me connect with others?

For those of us with faith in God, we know that God will help us. We slow down to become aware of His love and He helps us get connected with what is going on inside. Mark discussed in chapter 10 the importance of bringing God into the process. Clearly, our human nature recoils from self-awareness, yet the Bible counsels us to examine our hearts, motives, attitudes, and actions.

This first step of connecting is the most important, but often the most overlooked.

Maria has a friend that suggests she take some time out to process the situation, as she is losing sleep. The friend offers to walk with her through the steps and they start with taking a few deep breaths and say a simple prayer. "God, can you help me process this situation."

Tips for Step #1 - Connect

- Understand the importance of slowing down to connect in order to get clarity.

- Remember the times you have stopped to connect with God that have helped you break free of defeating patterns. This will come in time. Reinforcing the "wins" is the best motivation to stay in the game.

- Remember the times you neglected processing and experienced more relational problems that ended up consuming more time!

Am I willing to slow down and do what it takes to make better choices?

Caution: Two tendencies in reflection

Before we move to step two consider the two tendencies that get us off track.

1. We get stuck in remorse and self-condemnation. We feel so bad for our mistakes, and we feel paralyzed.

2. We are too quick and shallow, missing areas of our thoughts, feelings, and behavior.

These two tendencies are signs we have not stopped to connect. We have not slowed down and taken a deep breath to let our physiological state relax so we can use our brains properly. Don't skip the first step!

Step #2 – Clarify

Now that we are calmer, we can look at what is going on inside that is driving our feelings and actions? Clarity is another word for awareness. If we do not discern the factors of what is actually going on, we will miss the value that can be gained. **If you skip this step** and make changes before understanding what is going on underneath, you might make things worse.

Maria's friend asked her three simple questions:

a) How do you view this situation?

b) How do you think the other person viewed the situation?

c) How do you think God sees the situation?

Tips for Step #2 - Clarify

- Be specific. What were *my* thoughts, feelings, and actions?

- What may the *other person's* thoughts, feelings and actions have been? How I view the other person involved is crucial. This questions will reveal if we have judgements and assumptions of the other person.

- Writing out your answers can help you to be thorough. If you do not like writing in a journal, try making a list in point form.

Step #3 – Consider

Now that you have clarity regarding the three perspectives of the situation, go a little deeper by asking more questions. You might think of this step as taking all the information you gained in the clarity step and filtering it down to capture what is most important. Have you ever seen a person mining for gold? They take volumes of water and debris into a funnel and let the non-essentials drain out, so they have only the gold left. This step is where you mine the gold.

Maria's friend asked her:

a) What was happening inside of you that led to your actions?

b) What might have been happening in the other person?

c) What do you want most for this relationship?

Tips for Step #3 - Consider

- Remind yourself to stay connected through the whole process

- Sometimes it helps to step outside and take a brief walk or change rooms.

- Observe if there a pattern you see in yourself, this relationship, or other relationships?

- Consider if you need a qualified person to help you see what you might be missing? If you are struggling with these questions, consider finding a wise and trustworthy person to process with. Do not look for an ally that will just make you feel better. You need insight in order to be thorough in the repair of this relationship. Objectify the situation from as many angles as possible.

Step #4 – Choose

This step is where you use what you have learned to make an informed choice. All of life is about choices. Even when we decide not to make a choice, we are making a choice. We are either moving toward healthy relationships and peace or moving away from them.

Once we understand our part and what the other person experienced, we are better equipped to make the changes necessary.

Maria's friend asked her two questions:

a) What action will help rebuild and strengthen this relationship?

b) What is one thing you can do to rebuild trust and not repeat the same mistake?

Tips for Step #4 - Choose

- Make a list of all the options you can think of to strengthen the relationship.

- Plan and take the first step.

- Revisit this process in a few weeks. That is another reason it is helpful to write your thoughts out.

Personal example:

I am a recovering interrupter. I desperately want to avoid being misunderstood and often speak in the middle of people's sentences if I felt they were misreading me in any way.

The habit of interrupting a person in conversation can lead to frustrations and misunderstandings. This may seem minor, but it is a habit that needs to be replaced with listening skills.

In order to bring lasting remedy to the damage this was causing, I asked my husband to help me. As we talked I became aware of the fear I have of being misunderstood. We worked out a cue of taking a deep breath before a conversation so that I was calmer. Then he asked me how he was doing on interrupting. As we talked through the process we discovered that he often had a helpful insight that would help me before, I was done describing my situation. That was great, but I wasn't thinking for myself. I started to rely on his thoughts. So we worked out a phrase,

"I am happy to hear your insights when I have finished describing my situation, but if you interrupt, I will need to start at the beginning again."

Works every time.

When you use these steps to process a situation, your relationships will be stronger and more fruitful. These steps and questions are broad enough to be personal to you and your situation. Everyone is unique and therefore all situations are unique.

ESSENTIAL SKILLS TO STRENGTHEN RELATIONSHIPS

The best thing about mistakes is they can help us grow our relational skill set. Part of all remedy is learning from our mistakes and being accountable to develop better skills. When we do this, we not only show others we take relationships seriously, but we avoid repeating the same mistakes.

1. Learn to give an effective apology

2. Learn to invite feedback

3. Learn to have crucial conversations

4. Learn to communicate clearly

The worksheets provided in "The Boss is Dead Companion workbook" will provide helpful tips and a template to use to increase skills in each of these areas. The following provides a sample of some options.

1. Learn to give an effective apology

Have you ever had someone think they were apologizing, when in reality all they were doing was justifying what they did? They ended up creating more insult and injury. There is a better way. Take the time to think through an apology before you give it using the four steps: connect, clarify, consider, and choose. We suggest you write out your apology to help organize your thoughts, but deliver your apology in person. A letter is the last resource. Some people feel writing it out is not necessary, but it is. You may only get one chance at an apology, so it is better to do thorough preparation.

After you have used the four steps to process the situation internally, use the same four steps to deliver the apology.

a) Connect – Ask the person if this is a good time for them to discuss something important. Tell them your connection with them is valuable and you want to preserve and strengthen it.

b) Clarify – State your specific action and take responsibility without giving explanations. Don't use "ifs, ands and buts." These words result in a conditional apology which is really no apology at all. "I would not have done what I did **if** you had not done..."

c) Consider - Listen to the person. Let them fully express themselves without interrupting to explain your side. Repeat back to them to show them you understand. Our temptation is to avoid the pain of hearing the discomfort and assume we know how this affected them. There is a high likelihood that the person's perspective will be skewed, and you will want to clarify. Hang in there, if you try to clarify too soon, you are not giving an effective apology. *This is about how they felt.* The key is to remember the process and not try to rush things.

d) Choose - Let them know what change you are able to make to prevent a repeat of the offense and rebuild any trust that was lost. Not all mistakes are equal because not all people are alike. We have different personalities, histories, needs and wants. The harm that was done affects each person in a unique way, it was personal. Therefore, the remedy needs to be unique and personal as well.

Consider the following two examples. Which would you prefer?

Charles was feeling good that he had completed his reflection and planned a proper apology to do shortly after his mistake. What he didn't consider was what his mistake had cost his son. Charles was determined to get the apology over with and go on with life. Afterall, we all make mistakes, and his son needs to learn to forgive.

"It was hard to listen as a young girl (more than half my age) outlined my faults. It would have been easy to dismiss her comments because she was so angry and didn't understand the full picture. And yet, I thought, wait a minute... there is always something I can learn. Perhaps I can change my attitude and benefit from this conversation no matter how it is delivered?"

2. Learn to invite feedback

We are going to get feedback whether we want it or not. Wouldn't it be better to invite feedback on a regular basis rather than wait until someone's frustration has peaked? There is a significant difference between inviting feedback and hearing feedback mixed with frustration.

Benefits:

- We are less likely to be defensive when we are prepared.

- It is one of the only blind spots remedy. We all have areas in our life where we don't see how we are affecting others. We call these blind spots. The only way to grow past your blind spots is to request feedback on a consistent basis. People aren't likely to speak about your blind spots unless you invite them.

- Relationships last longer and are stronger. Most people will withdraw from a relationship rather than address any unpleasant issues. Or if they can't withdraw, they let their frustration with your blind spot accumulate until they blow up in anger. Both extremes can be avoided by regularly requesting feedback from those you are in relationship with.

Tips re: feedback

a) Connect – Before I invite feedback I like to ask this question: *What benefit could I derive from feedback if I was willing to put my pride and ego aside? Am I ready?*

b) Clarify – Tell a person close to you about your desire for feedback and the reasons why. Ask them if they could give some feedback within the next 2 weeks. It is easier for them to have some time. Ask if they would observe a specific area (i.e. your tendency to be defensive) and also anything else they observe.

c) Consider – Take a few days to consider the feedback they give. The point is not to judge if they were right or wrong. The information provides you how they viewed the situation and how that can help you in your relationship with them and perhaps others.

d) Choose – Decide what actions would be helpful in light of the information you received. Follow up with the person who gave you feedback a few weeks later.

For example, my husband and I will say to each other at least once a month, "Hey there, I am just checking in. How am I doing in our relationship?" Often, we will mention the specific adjustment we are working on. For example, "Am I getting better at not interrupting?"

"Feedback is not only the breakfast of champions, but the lunch, dinner, and snacks as well." Ken Blanchard

3. Learn to have crucial conversations

A crucial conversation is a discussion between two or more people where: (a) stakes are high, (b) opinions vary, and (c) emotions run strong.

There has been a lot written about how to have a successful crucial conversation. Still, many of us would rather avoid the unpleasantness and accept a superficial relationship. The more we choose to avoid crucial conversations the smaller our world becomes.

When we settle for superficial relationships, the *quality* of ALL our relationships will suffer. If we are in leadership, we may experience a high staff turnover because people want something better. People crave purpose and meaning, and not being willing to have difficult conversations affects all of your relationships.

a) Connect – Ask the person if you could have some time with them for an important conversation.

b) Clarify – State in a short and concise way what you feel the issue is from your vantage point and that you would like to understand their perspective.

c) Consider – Pause to repeat back what you heard and discuss some implications for both of you.

d) Choose – Discuss what a good action could result from what you learned together.

Tips re: crucial communication:

• Practice. There is no substitute for practicing. We learn by doing.

• One idea of how to practice is to let a friend or coworker know you are working on improving your crucial conversations skills and ask if you can do practice "role-play" with them. Pick a topic or situation and practice your skill in talking about something crucial.

- The more you practice, prepare and process, the better experiences you will have.

- Your confidence and competence grow with practice. Don't wait for confidence; practice and gain it.

4. Learn to give clear communication

Often relationship mistakes occur when we haven't been clear and straight forward in our communication. We are often running at a fast pace and have made many assumptions. Slowing down may take time at the beginning but will save you many problems in the long run.

When we clearly tell people what works and doesn't work for us, we are communicating a "*boundary*." We avoid problems when we look at what is going to strengthen the relationship.

A *boundary* is a term used to bring clarity and to preserve a relationship. **It is about *us*** – not *you* or *them*.

Many of us haven't taken the time to understand our boundaries and limits, although we do know when they have been crossed. We experience frustration and sometimes anger. We are surprised they didn't *know better*!

Story of Maria - Example of communicating clearly:

a) Connect – Maria was appreciative of her friend helping her explore the situation with her daughter. She decided to take some time to organize her thoughts to be able to communicate clearly with her daughter. She wanted some place quiet, so she took her car to a favorite spot and parked. She took some deep breaths, asked God for help, and got settled with a piece of paper to make some

267

notes. She had notes from before, but she wanted to start with a fresh piece of paper.

b) Clarify – She made a list of what she wanted in her relationship with her daughter. Things like peace, joy, good communication, trust, fun. She also made a list of some limitations such as her daughter's busy schedule, fluctuating hormones for both of them, some bad experiences trying to communicate, and Maria's difficult childhood. It was helpful to write down what she wanted, as well as and what she didn't want.

c) Consider – As Maria looked at the lists, she realized how much the limitations of bad experiences trying to communicate, and her own difficult childhood, were affecting her. She remembered a counselor she had seen and made a note to give her a call. She also thought it would be helpful to communicate her hopes for a better relationship with her daughter. She knew with the schedule challenges; it would be best to select a time that worked for her daughter. She remembered they used to go out for their favorite coffee together. It was interesting for her to note that when she was calm, and had time to process the situation, she found herself remembering good times with her daughter. She realized there was more to their relationship than the unpleasant discussion and tension.

d) Choose – Maria decided to do a practice recording on her phone of a conversation with her daughter. She would feel more confident that way. Here is what she said in her practice:

Hi honey, do you have a few minutes. I want to set up a time that works for both of us to go for our favorite coffee. Is there a time that would work?

Then Maria practiced what she would say when they went out. She could use the same four steps. *I am glad we got to do this together. I wanted to connect. I have been thinking what could help us have more peace and fun together. I realized I was letting many of my fears and unpleasant memories affect our relationship and I am working through those things so that our relationship can be better. What do you think of setting a time each week we can go out for coffee. Just for fun. Nothing heavy. We can put the heavy topics on hold and just enjoy relaxing together. I really like you and I think this will help. What do you think?*

Summary and final tips:

Our goal is to maintain and build connection in relationships.

We focus on growth not perfection. An expectation of perfection makes relationships a chore. Humility and courage are fantastic travel partners as we pursue healthy connection in all our relationships.

- Mistakes mean you are doing something – you are moving. The more you take the stigma out of mistakes the more you can face the truth and move forward.

- Mistakes can give you helpful information, but they do not define you.

- Take the time to process the mistake so it doesn't drain your confidence, joy, and future decisions.

- Understand the difference between ruminating and connecting to reflect. Ruminating is going over and over something and never taking an action to move forward. Connecting helps us move forward.

- Let go of trying to be perfect, but rather choose to be a person who is learning and growing. An expectation of perfection makes relationships a chore. Humility and courage are fantastic travel partners as we pursue healthy connection in all our relationships.

- Keep a gratitude journal. This gives you balance so you don't get stuck in negative thinking.

- Get back in the game as soon as possible. Our goal is to continually strengthen the connection in all our relationships.

The companion workbook available for this book provides practical ways to grow and develop your relational skill set.

Some Questions to Consider:

1. Which of the four steps [connect, clarify, consider, and choose] do you find you do well?

2. Describe your thoughts regarding the four skills for strengthening relationships. [learn to give an effective apology, invite feedback, have crucial conversations, and clear communication.]

3. Which of the guidelines do you find most helpful regarding making an effective apology?

4. What is one take-away from this chapter you can apply right away?

Chapter 22: Is The Boss Really Dead?

As I stated in the introduction, it would be very easy to assume, based upon the weaknesses of positional leadership set out in this book, that I am arguing for the death of positional leadership. This is not the case.

A scene from an old Monty Python movie comes to mind. The scene is set in medieval England during the plague. A scruffy worker is pushing a cart through the village shouting, "bring out your dead, bring out your dead." A man comes out of his cottage carrying another man over his shoulder. Obviously, he intends depositing the man onto the cart for burial. The problem is that the man is not dead yet.

An argument ensues between the cart driver and the resident who wants to get rid of the man he is claiming as dead. The cart driver rightly objects that he cannot take the man while he is still alive. The "dead" guy joins in the argument claiming that he is not dead yet, to which the man carrying him answers, "yes, but you are not at all well are you?"

Positional leadership is not at all well

Positional leadership is still very much alive, but it is not at all well. It is under siege on all fronts in the Western World. This should not be the case. The Bible tells us clearly to obey our leaders:

"Have confidence in your leaders and submit to their authority, because they keep watch over you as those who must give an account. Do this so that their work will be a joy, not a burden, for that would be of no benefit to you." Hebrews 13:17

The word "burden" used here could be translated as "a deep groan." Many times, as a leader I have experienced just such a deep groan, as have all parents, teachers, coaches, etc. The Bible tells us that when we discourage our leaders, we rob ourselves of the benefits God intended for us through their leadership.

Although the Bible tells us to obey our leaders, and we should, it spends far more time telling leaders how they should lead. This fact suggests that positional leadership alone will not accomplish what God has designed leadership to accomplish. We need to limit the abuses of positional leadership in order to derive the most benefit from it. And this is what this book set out to do.

We need to limit the abuses of positional leadership in order to derive the most benefit from it.

The question remains, when is positional leadership necessary and beneficial? My short answer is "when every other kind of leadership has been tried and found inadequate." The sad fact is that there are those whose wounds are beyond our ability to overcome, no matter how well we lead. Jesus was the best servant leader who ever lived, yet He had to let Judas go to his fate unchanged.

Simply occupying a place of leadership exposes us to those who have been hurt by past leadership and who are not ready to "have confidence in their leader and submit to their authority." Admitting that fact and releasing them with grace is not a failure to lead. You cannot lead someone who does not want to be led. Yet, this should not be our "go to" excuse for a failure to lead through influence.

When is positional leadership our first choice?

So, what sorts of problems call for strong positional leadership? Some obvious situations come to mind:

1. Emergencies and time sensitive decisions.

Emergencies do not lend themselves to committee discussions or time taken to explore the self-awareness issues that might bear on the ultimate decision. In an emergency, someone must take charge and act decisively.

Where a matter is time sensitive [e.g. the church needs a bookkeeper in order to fulfill IRS requirements which have to be done immediately] someone will have to make the decision as to who to hire NOW.

2. Where the leadership is equally divided on an issue.

Take the last example. The board is equally divided between two possible bookkeepers. A decision must be made. Either they flip a coin, or the positional leader should decide.

3. In matters of unrepentant sin.

My bias is clearly in favor of acting in grace wherever possible. I will hang in with a person struggling with sin as long as he is giving a shred of effort to change. Sometimes, such grace is not enough to bring repentance, and tough love becomes divine mercy. When this happens, it is the role of the positional leader to enforce the hard decision. Church discipline exists in the Bible because unrepentant sin exists in the church. However, before taking such a radical step, every skill of influential leadership should be exhausted.

Sometimes, such grace is not enough to bring repentance, and tough love becomes divine mercy.

I am sure there are other situations that call for positional leadership, but the point of this book is not to exhaustively answer that question. My goal is to correct what has been a historical and theological bias towards largely exclusive positional leadership within the church, business, government, the family, and our society as a whole. Our human nature favors positional leadership because our human nature is "fallen." It will always be our "natural" default position. By God's grace we can overcome this bias and learn to become people of influence. The reward is worth the effort.

"You have been faithful with a few things; I will put you in charge of many things. Come and share your master's happiness!' Matt. 25: 21

Final thought

Let me end this book with a final thought. All of us, in one situation or another, are in a situation in which we are either leading or following. At home I might be leading my family, but at work I might be following my boss. When we get to heaven, we are going to be judged for how well we led in those moments in which we were supposed to lead.

As well, we will be judged for how well we followed in those moments in which we were supposed to follow. Both how we led and how we followed are eternally important to God, and to our enjoyment of heaven. Good leadership matters!

I pray that this book will help you to be a better leader. I invite you to be a part of an ongoing conversation about influential leadership. Feel free to join us for that conversation at www.mark.cowpersmith.org

Chapter 23: What Have We Learned?

Let's review the chapters of the book to summarize what we have learned.

SECTION ONE – HOW THE BOSS BECAME THE BOSS

1. Our Western culture is rapidly changing. We are living in an age of growing disrespect for positional authority. This culture of disrespect has infected all of the institutions of our secular society. It has also infected the Church. A shift toward leadership through influence provides hope for the leadership of the future.

2. Positional Authority is God's design for the governance of His creation. He delegated positional authority to mankind and allows the redelegation of it from leader to leader. Although God ordained positional leadership, He chose leaders who:

   a. Did not seek positional leadership,
   b. He supernaturally confirmed His call to, &
   c. Had a conversational relationship with God throughout their term of leadership.

Those leaders who met these three characteristics prospered and so did Israel under their leadership. Sadly, this kind of godly leader was rare. The history of Old Testament Israel is largely the history of failed positional leadership. The examples of godly leadership in this chapter are Moses, Joshua and Gideon.

3. In this chapter we looked at Samuel and the Kings of Israel. Samuel followed in the three characteristics of godly leadership found in chapter two. Because of the failure of Samuel's sons as leaders, the people of Israel demanded a king. God warned

Israel about the abuses that having a king would bring to them. God was opposed to the institution of kingship, but He gave them what they asked for. We examined four kings of note, both good and bad. They are Saul, David, Absalom, & Solomon. We found that those who conformed to the pattern of Moses [as found in chapter two] prospered, and those that did not were terrible failures. We also found that the nation rode the coattails of the king for better or for worse.

4. We examined the Good, Bad, and Ugly of Positional Leadership through the lives of those leaders found in chapter three. The following observations were made.

   a. *Unfettered power is corrupting most of the time.*

   b. *Positional Leadership provides a good hiding place from personal blind spots, sin, insecurity, accountability, etc.*

   c. *Positional Leadership promote a false self-worth and hence attracts the insecure. It ensures they are likely to remain unchallenged in their insecurity.*

   d. *Positional Leadership promotes and rewards a sycophant culture.*

   e. *Positional Leadership is good for times of war and bad for times of peace.*

   f. *The Positional Leader's relationship with God becomes the "God experience" of the people. When the leader is godly the people experience blessing. Conversely, when the leader is ungodly the people experience judgement. The latter is by far the most common.*

5. When Israel rejected an intimate relationship with God at Mt. Sinai, they were given life under the Law. Behavior is either motivated internally [from the heart] or externally through either force or reward. [Law] Positional leadership requires laws to enforce its leadership hence, leadership under the Law in the Old Testament was positional. This was not God's will but was rather a consequence of rejecting the internal

motivation of an intimate relationship of love with a loving God. Positional Leadership became institutionalized with the establishment of the Law.

SECTION TWO – THE NEW DEAL

6. The New Covenant not only brought freedom from punishment for sin through forgiveness, it also brought the indwelling of the Holy Spirit to every believer. The indwelling Holy Spirit became the internal motivator that replaced the external motivator. [the Law] This necessitates a difference type of leadership. Leadership under grace is predominantly through influence rather than positional authority. We see this exemplified in the leadership of Jesus.

7. The Apostle Paul avoided using positional authority whenever possible. He led through influence via persuasion and love.

SECTION THREE: CHARACTERISTICS OF INFLUENTIAL LEADERSHIP

8. Competence is the least effective means of acquiring influence, yet it is the factor most pursued by many leaders. Competence discussed includes 1] Good Bible teaching, 2] Good Administration, 3] Financial Success, 4] Advanced Education, 5] Spiritual Giftedness, & 6] Compelling Vision

9. Character is the second most important means of acquiring influence. Character discussed includes humility, having a servant's heart, integrity, honesty & authenticity.

10. Internal Self-Awareness involves the accurate understanding of one's deepest desires, needs, dreams, strengths and weaknesses. Without it we lead with blind spots

which sabotage our relationships with those we lead. External Self-Awareness involves the accurate understanding of how others perceive those same things within us. Without knowing how others are perceiving us we cannot lead them well.

11. Emotional Intelligence involves how well we manage our own difficult emotions and the difficult emotions of those we lead. Without mature emotional intelligence we act out of negative emotions which brings disrespect from those we lead, resulting in less influential leadership.

12. On the survey I did regarding what factors bring greater influence to a leader, leading by example was near the top of the list. Leading by example is an act of integrity which brings great influence to a leader. Related to leading by example is using teachable moments to train, rather than the easier but less effective classroom lecture model. Jesus taught through teachable moments almost exclusively.

13. Security in the love of the Father is essential to becoming a leader of influence. Leadership attracts often harsh criticism which breeds insecurity. Without a source of security that goes deeper than job success, a leader will ride an emotional roller coaster of highs and lows which will be obvious to those he leads. This display of instability undermines the followers' confidence in the leader, hence robbing the leader of influence. Time spent in intimacy with God is the antidote for insecurity.

14. Leading from love was the most important factor named by those who completed my leadership survey. We explore the example of how God leads us as a good "father." We then look at how Jesus led His disciples as a "friend." Both of these roles when applied to those we lead result in greater influence.

15. Asking good questions of those we lead is an act of love. It not only shows our interest in them as a person, but it also

gives us the opportunity to help them navigate the difficult situations they find themselves in.

16. Jesus asked approximately 175 questions within the four gospels. It was His preferred method of teaching His disciples. He asked great questions. We looked at His most common questions to discover why they are so important.

17. Having looked at Jesus' example of asking good questions, we explored how to ask good questions. This chapter is a purely practical discussion of how questions can be used to guide those we lead.

18. The choice of what question to ask next depends on the answer to the last one. This means that really listening well is hugely important to the questioning process. Not only that but, listening well is an act of love. To love is to listen and to listen is to love. This chapter becomes a practical guide as to how to listen well. Listening well brings great influence to a leader.

19. Too many visionary leaders put their vision ahead of the people they lead. They end up using people, which results in high job turnover and premature exits. A vision is best served by serving those who serve the vision. We explore how a leader can make the people the vision without sacrificing his vision.

20. Every follower comes with a personal vision. A visionary leader who takes the time to identify his followers' personal visions has the opportunity to find a place for them within his vision, which place will allow for the fulfilment of their personal vision. People whose personal vision is fulfilled in their job are productive workers and happy people. Their loyalty is huge. As well in this chapter, we look at the effect in the workplace, and team, of celebrating the success of each team member.

21. We are bound to make mistakes. Learning how to repair and reconnect relationships is crucial. In order to break out of the dysfunctional cycles we get in, each person needs to start with themselves. Understanding that we are the only person that we can control is crucial. It starts with each of us making significant changes in our thinking. We can learn what is needed.

22. After reading an entire book dedicated to replacing command and control with influence it is easy to reach the conclusion that positional authority should be rejected entirely. This is not a valid conclusion. Positional authority remains necessary in many situations. We explore these and reach the conclusion that striving for influence should be our norm and using our positional authority should be the exception.

22. As for "What have we learned?" you just read it.

Footnotes:

Chapter 1:

#1. Matthew Harrington, Harvard Business Review, Jan. 16th, 2017, Title?

#2. Dhruv Khullar, entitled "Do You Trust the Medical Profession? Profession?" The New York Times January 23, 2018

#3. Reluctantly Supernatural In an Age of Reason, Mark Cowper-Smith and Bob Maddux, Kindle Publishing Oct 28, 2019

#4. LinkedIn article by Brigette Hyacinth, author of 1. The Future of Leadership: Rise of Automation, Robotics and Artificial Intelligence, 2. The Ultimate Leader: Learning, Leading and Leaving a Legacy of Hope, 3. The Edge of Leadership: A Leader's Handbook for Success
"Employees don't leave Companies, they leave Managers." Dec. 17, '17

Chapter 2:

#5. Reluctantly Supernatural In an Age of Reason, Mark Cowper-Smith and Bob Maddux, Kindle Publishing Oct 28, 2019 - P. 138

#6 Reluctantly Supernatural In an Age of Reason, Mark Cowper-Smith and Bob Maddux, Kindle Publishing Oct 28, 2019

Chapter 4:

#7. James O'Toole, quoted in Harvard Business Review, Jan. 4, '18 "What Self-Awareness Really is (and How to Cultivate It) Tasha Eurich, organizational psychologist

#8. Tasha Eurich, Harvard Business Review, Jan. 4, '18 "What Self-awareness Really is Self-Awareness [And how to Cultivate it] (and How to Cultivate It) Tasha Eurich, organizational psychologist

#9. Ibid

#10. [Article: Harvard Business School, Working Knowledge: Business Research for Business Leaders, 06 June 2011, Research and Ideas, "Why Leaders Lose Their Way" by Bill George]

#11. Business Week New York, Nov. 3 2003 - Iss. 3856 p. 76

Chapter 5:

#12. Dallas Willard, Renovation of the Heart, Navpress, NavPress, 2002, p. 15

#13. Ibid

#14. Mark Cowper-Smith, [Paraphrased from Reluctantly Supernatural p. 225-228] Reluctantly Supernatural In an Age of Reason, Mark Cowper-Smith and Bob Maddux, Kindle Publishing Oct 28, 2019

Chapter 6:

#15. Pastor Erwin R. McManus, pastor, Mosaic Church, Los Angeles, Servant Leadership in Action, Edited by Ken Blanchard and Rene Broadwell, Berrett Koehler, 2018 p. 131

#16. Francis Frangipane, House United, Chosen Books, 2005, p. 123

Chapter 8:

#17. President Calvin Coolidge, from a talk in January 1925 to the Society of American Newspaper Editors in Washington, D. C.

#18. Erwin Raphael McManus, pastor Mosaic Church LA. Servant Leadership in Action, Edited by Ken Blanchard and Rene Broadwell, Berrett Koehler, 2018 p. 129

Chapter 9:

#19. James M. Kouzes and Dr. Barry Posner, Finding Your Voice, Servant Leadership in Action, Edited by Ken Blanchard and Rene Broadwell, Berrett Koehler, 2018 p. 110, 111, 113

#20. T.J. Addington, Deep Influence, NavPress, 2014, p. 98

#21. Daniel Coyle, author of the book "Culture Code." https://www.successpodcast.com/show-notes/2018/10/17/the-hidden-brain-science-that-will-unlock-your-true-potential-with-daniel-coyle

Chapter 10:

#22. https://www.theguardian.com/science/2014/jul/03/electric-shock-preferable-to-thinking-says-study

#23. Tasha Eurich and her associates, entitled What Self-Awareness Really Is (and How to Cultivate It) in the Harvard Business Review, Jan 2018.

#24. Ibid

#25. Ibid

Chapter 11:

#26. T.J. Addington, Deep Influence, Navpress, NavPress, 2014, p. 117

#27. Ibid. p. 119

#28. Ibid. p. 122

#29. Ibid. p. 123

#30 Ibid. p. 125

#31. Ibid. p. 128

#32. Ibid. p. 128

Chapter 12:

#33. Mark Miller, from Chick-fil-A, Servant Leadership in Action, Edited by Ken Blanchard and Rene Broadwell, Berrett Koehler, 2018, p. 36

#34. Dave Ramsey, Ibid, p. 198

Chapter 14

#35. Eddie L. Hyatt, Pursuing Power, Hyatt Press, 2014, p. 6

#36. The Blessing, Gary Smalley and John Trent, Nelson Incorporated, Thomas 2004

#37. Martyn Lloyd Jones, Romans 8, Banner of Truth

Chapter 15

#38. David Hoffeld, [CEO and chief sales trainer at Hoffeld Group, [The Science of Work, Feb. 21, 2017 "What To Know What Your Brain Does When It Hears a Question?" Fast Company web site. His book is "The Science of Selling: Proven Strategies to Make Your Pitch, Influence Decisions, & Close the Deal." TarcherPerigee, an imprint of Penguin Publishing Group, a division of Penguin Random House LCC. Copyright c. 2016]

#39. [PNAS Proceedings of the National Academy of Sciences of the United States of America, "Disclosing information about the self is intrinsically rewarding" Diana I. Tamir & Jason P. Mitchell, PNAS May 22, 2012, 109 [21] 8038 – 8043]

Chapter 16:

#40 Dale Roach, Article: – Like a Team, A Christian Resource for Leadership and Teamwork Development, Blog site, blog post, [see also, The Servant Leadership Style of Jesus by Dale Roach]

Chapter 18:

#41. David Oxberg
at: http://www.thecoachingtoolscompany.com/39-of-the-most-beautiful-quotes-about-love-handpicked-for-you/#sthash.QkPsBKFS.dpuf

#42. Paul Tillich
at: http://www.thecoachingtoolscompany.com/39-of-the-most-beautiful-quotes-about-love-handpicked-for-you/#sthash.QkPsBKFS.dpuf

#43. Erik Barker "Barking Up the Wrong Tree" "How to be Loved by Everyone: 6 Powerful Secrets"

#44 Linda Miller and Chad Hall, Coaching for Christian Leaders, A practical guide, Chalice Press, 2007

#45. Dietrich Bonhoeffer, Life Together published post-humus [Harper & Row, Publishers, Inc. 1954], p. 97

Chapter 19:

#46. Ibid. p. 99

Chapter 20:

#47. Tom Mullins author of The Leadership Game, [Nashville: Thomas Nelson, 2005], Servant Leadership in Action, Edited by

Ken Blanchard and Rene Broadwell, Berrett Koehler, 2018, p. 77

#48. Ibid. p. 79

#49. Ibid. p. 80

Appendix 1

Old Testament Positional Leadership

Moses

Moses is the prototypical leader of the Old Testament. He is a type and foreshadowing of Jesus. He said of himself,

"The Lord your God will raise up for you a prophet like me from among your own people; you shall heed such a prophet." Deut. 18:15

He is of course prophesying the prophetic ministry of Jesus. I have written on this elsewhere, so I will just quote myself:

"Moses exemplified God's plan for His leadership over His people. God's leadership mechanism in the Old Testament was a man who was prophet, priest and governor in one leader. In other words, these three roles operating in unity comprised God's design for leadership. Sadly, this unity came to an end. Gradually three distinct functions or traditions began to form: Prophets, Priests and Kings.

The divide accelerated when Israel demanded a king. The story is quite simple. Israel was a theocracy surrounded by nations ruled by a king. Israel was the odd man out. The peoples' reaction was predictable, "Everyone else has a king, so we should have a king too." One of Satan's greatest lies is this; "Everyone else is doing it, so you should too." The people took the bait and began demanding a king.

They presented their demands to their prophet Samuel who took the matter to God. Samuel was not pleased.

"But the thing displeased Samuel when they said, 'Give us a king to govern us.' Samuel prayed to the Lord, and the Lord said to Samuel, 'Listen to the voice of the people in all that they say to you; for they have not rejected you, but they have rejected me from being king over them'" 1 Sam. 8:6.

It is important to note that it is not the choice of who will be king that God objects to - it is the institution of kingship that God does not want. (1 Sam. 10:19) It is after Israel's rejection of God's form of leadership that we see the separation of the three functions of leadership. From this point onward, we see an almost constant struggle between the three institutions of prophet, priest and king. It is within this separation that the Old Testament role of prophet becomes one of opposition, not just to bad kings, but to the institution of kingship itself. (Hosea 8:4; Amos 5:26)" Reluctantly Supernatural in an Age of Reason, p.152

The purpose of this book is not a discussion of the animosity between prophets, priests and kings in the Old Testament. Our present concern is an examination of positional leadership in the Old Testament and for this we will make a closer examination of Moses' positional leadership.

A Supernatural Call to Leadership

The first characteristic to note concerns the means through which God calls Moses into leadership. God reveals Himself to Moses supernaturally. Moses encounters a flaming bush that will not burn up. Even more supernatural, the bush speaks to him! The voice of God emanates from the bush! Here is overwhelming evidence for Moses to believe that he is hearing the genuine voice of God. One would think that such an experience would fill Moses with the faith necessary to agree to taking the leadership role God is about to call him to. Not so!

A Reluctance to Lead

God tells Moses to go back to Egypt to confront Pharaoh and then to lead the people of Israel out of Egypt. What God is offering Moses is a place in history alongside Abraham, but Moses doesn't want the honor saying,

"Who am I, that I should go to Pharaoh and bring the Israelites out of Egypt?" Exodus 3:11

Moses then argues with God to avoid God's leadership assignment. God's response is to perform the "staff to snake and back again miracle." Still Moses argues that he is a terrible public speaker, and that God should find someone else. God suggests Aaron as Moses' public relations agent and so Moses, having run out of excuses, agrees to become the foremost leader of the Old Testament.

The second and most important characteristic of Moses positional leadership is that he does not seek it, in fact, he tries to avoid it. Herein lies one of the secrets to successful positional leadership. Those who want it least are the ones who are usually not corrupted by it. Positional leadership is essentially the right, by virtue of the position alone, to command whatever the leader wishes. The command does not have to be explained or justified. The potential for the abuse of power is extreme because the authority is absolute. Lord Acton's principle comes to mind, "power corrupts, and absolute power corrupts absolutely."

A Conversational Relationship with God

288

The third characteristic of Moses' positional leadership is that it is relational. Moses begins a conversational relationship with God from the first moment, and it lasts throughout his entire leadership career. The importance of a positional leader being in an intimate relationship with God cannot be overstated. It is this relationship that keeps the leader safe, both for his own spiritual survival and for the good of those he leads. As we examine positional leadership throughout the Old Testament, we will see this truth confirmed again and again.

Joshua

Joshua was God's choice to succeed Moses. Joshua's call into positional leadership contains the same three characteristics as Moses'. Joshua was witness to all the supernatural miracles God performed through Moses while Israel crossed the desert to the promised land. He also led the attack against Jericho in which God reduced the mighty walls of the city to rubble while the warriors of Israel did nothing but worship. That's supernatural!

> The importance of a positional leader being in an intimate relationship with God cannot be overstated. It is this relationship that keeps the leader safe, both for his own spiritual survival and for the good of those he leads.

Like Moses, Joshua did not attempt to assume leadership, he merely responded to the voice of God. He did not covet a leadership role, God thrust it upon him.

Like Moses, he too had a conversational relationship with God. More than 17 times in the book of Joshua we find God and Joshua in conversation.

Gideon

After the nation of Israel entered the promised land [Canaan] we find a period of national decline. God gave very specific instruction about remaining separate, both religiously and socially, from the pagan cultures and inhabitants of the conquered land. Despite this, Israel ignored His commands and adopted the idolatry of the false religions surrounding it. As well, Israel engaged in the forbidden practice of intermarriage, which further angered God. God's response was swift; He withdrew His hand of protection. Calamity and suffering followed for Israel in the form of subservience to the very nations they had just conquered.

This period of Israel's history is referred to as the time of the "Judges." The period was characterized by Israel's apostacy, leading to subservience, leading to desperation, leading to God's deliverance through "judges." These judges were raised up by God as military leaders to go to war to liberate Israel. Soon after God's liberation, the nation would again forget God's commands and the cycle of decline and deliverance would begin again.

During this period, Israel's success depended on the leadership qualities of the judges. Sadly, for every good judge there seemed to soon follow a bad one, or a series of bad ones. Interestingly, the period of the judges, both for good and bad, is summed up by two judges: Gideon and his son Abimelech. Gideon is our example of a good judge.

Gideon began his tenure as a judge as did Moses, with a supernatural encounter. An angel of the Lord came to visit Gideon with a command to go and save Israel. The encounter is very similar to that between Moses and God.

"The Lord turned to him and said, "Go in the strength you have and save Israel out of Midian's hand. Am I not sending you?" "Pardon me, my lord," Gideon replied, "but how can I

save Israel? My clan is the weakest in Manasseh, and I am the least in my family." The LORD answered, "I will be with you, and you will strike down all the Midianites, leaving none alive." Judges 6:14-16

Like Moses, Gideon believed himself unqualified for the leadership position God was calling him to. Like Moses, Gideon required a supernatural sign, two in fact, to convince him of the wisdom of God's call. [Judges 6:36-40] Gideon had no ambition driving him to seek leadership, it was thrust upon him. After delivering Israel from oppression...

"The Israelites said to Gideon. "Rule over us – you, your son and your grandson – because you have saved us out of the hand of Midian." Judges 6:22

Gideon's response is clearly that he has no aspirations to a position of authority over the people. He answers them:

"I will not rule over you, nor will my son rule over you. The Lord will rule over you." Judges 6:23

Gideon, as well, had a conversational relationship with God. The story of Gideon's leadership is the working out of his conversations with God.

The only mistake Gideon made during his tenure as leader over Israel came because of greed. He requested and received from the plunder taken by his followers, 1700 shekels of gold. Today this would be worth more than a million dollars. He made the gold into an ephod which he displayed in his hometown. The result was probably not what he had in mind...

"All Israel prostituted themselves by worshiping it there, and it became a snare to Gideon and his family" Judges 8:27

The story of Gideon's leadership does not end well.

"No sooner had Gideon died than the Israelites again prostituted themselves to the Baals. They set up Baal-Berith as their god and did not remember the LORD their God, who had rescued them from the hands of all their enemies on every side." Judges 8:33-34 Judges 8:33-34

This is the pattern to be found in the story of positional leadership throughout the Old Testament. The spiritual health of the nation depends on the spiritual health of its leader. The writer of Judges emphasizes this fact with the use of the phrase "no sooner."

This pattern of rapid decay following the passing of a godly leader begs some very important questions. How can this happen so quickly? How can people being blessed by God turn from Him so thoroughly? What was going on within their hearts during the time they were "worshipping Him"? After we have finished our survey of positional leadership in the Old Testament we will return to these questions because the answer to these questions is the foundation for the model of leadership found in the New Testament. The answer is worth the wait.

Abimelech

To the degree Gideon's leadership was godly, Abimelech's was evil. Abimelech was one of Gideon's 70 sons. Yes, 70! Abimelech was Gideon's son with one of his concubines. Shortly after Gideon's death, Abimelech went to his 69 brothers and proposed to them that rather than share the leadership of Israel among all 70 of them, he should become the sole leader.

We should note that Abimelech is assuming that God has no choice in who is to follow Gideon's leadership. He is assuming that the succession common to the pagan cultures surrounding Israel should apply to Israel. This is a clear break from God's methodology. Abimelech ends his pitch for leadership to his 69 brothers with the argument that

"...remember that I am your flesh and blood." Judges 9:2

This will become important later in the story.

The brothers chose to support Abimelech in his bid for leader of Israel and advised the people accordingly, adding "he is our brother." [9:3] The people gave Abimelech 70 shekels of silver which he used to hire "reckless adventurers" as his followers. [9:4] With the help of his reckless adventurers he returned to his father's home where he murdered all but one of his brothers! So much for "family." The people of his hometown then crowned him as king.

Fortunately for our sense of justice, "what goes around comes around" for Abimelech. Three years later God allowed an evil spirit [probably a spirit of division or mistrust] to come between Abimelech and his followers. A usurper rose up to challenge Abimelech and a civil war ensued.

During this short war Abimelech set fire to a temple in which approximately 1000 men and women [probably including children] were hiding. They were all burned to death.

At the next town he attacked he found the inhabitants taking shelter in a strong tower. During his attempt to set the tower on fire a woman dropped a millstone from the roof. It hit Abimelech in the head and cracked his skull. Rather than admit that a woman had killed him he had his armor bearer kill him with a sword. [9:50-56]

The remainder of the book of Judges repeats the same story; good leaders followed by a string of bad leaders. A nation continually slipping from honoring God to quickly dishonoring Him, all depending on the spiritual state of the leader.

The book of Judges reveals Israel's error in coveting a king. Too much power in the hands of a king who neither knows God nor was chosen by Him is always a recipe for disaster. More than that, the institution of kingship was never God's plan for leading His people.

Appendix 2

Earn Your Paycheck By Listening First, Talking Later Guest Post by Gary A. Cohen

ABOUT THE AUTHOR

Gary A. Cohen

is an award-winning educator, teaching International Business and Global Trade Management to MBAs and Executive MBAs at the University of Maryland – Robert H. Smith School of Business. You can connect with Gary on LinkedIn.

Guest post from "Leading with Questions" with Bob Tiede,

"20 Questions Good Leaders Should Ask" Guest Post by Gary A. Cohen, March 04, 2019, Bob Tiede